COLLECTED WORKS OF RENÉ GUÉNON

THE KING OF THE WORLD

RENÉ GUÉNON

THE KING
OF THE WORLD

Translator
Henry D. Fohr

Edited by
Samuel D. Fohr

SOPHIA PERENNIS

HILLSDALE NY

Originally published in
French as *Le Roi du Monde*
© Éditions Gallimard 1958
English translation © Sophia Perennis 2001
Second Impression 2004

Series editor: James R. Wetmore

For information, address:
Sophia Perennis, P.O. Box 611
Hillsdale NY 12529
sophiaperennis.com

Library of Congress Cataloging-in-Publication Data

Guénon, René
[Roi du monde. English]
The King of the World / René Guénon ; translated by
Henry D. Fohr ; edited by Samuel D. Fohr

p. cm. — (Collected works of René Guénon)
Includes index.
ISBN 0 900588 54 3 (pbk: alk. paper)
ISBN 0 900588 58 6 (cloth: alk. paper)
1. Kings and rulers—Mythology. I. Fohr, S.D., 1943–
II. Title.
BL325.K5 G813 2001
291.2'13—dc21   2001000972

THE PUBLISHER
GIVES SPECIAL THANKS TO
HENRY D. AND JENNIE L. FOHR
FOR MAKING THIS EDITION POSSIBLE

CONTENTS

EDITORIAL NOTE

THE PAST CENTURY HAS WITNESSED an erosion of earlier cultural
values as well as a blurring of the distinctive characteristics of the
world's traditional civilizations, giving rise to philosophic and moral
relativism, multiculturalism, and dangerous fundamentalist reactions. As early as the 1920s, the French metaphysician René Guénon
(1886–1951) had diagnosed these tendencies and presented what he
believed to be the only possible reconciliation of the legitimate, although apparently conflicting, demands of outward religious forms,
'exoterisms', with their essential core, 'esoterism'. His works are char-
acterized by a foundational critique of the modern world coupled
with a call for intellectual reform; a renewed examination of metaphysics, the traditional sciences, and symbolism, with special reference to the ultimate unanimity of all spiritual traditions; and finally,
a call to the work of spiritual realization. Despite their wide influence, translation of Guénon's works into English has so far been
piecemeal. The *Sophia Perennis* edition is intended to fill the urgent
need to present them in a more authoritative and systematic form. A
complete list of Guénon's works, given in the order of their original
publication in French, follows this note.

The present book grew out of a conference called by the chief
editor of the prestigious journal *Les Nouvelles Littèraires* in 1924 to
discuss Ferdinand Ossendowski's then recently published *Beasts,
Men and Gods*. The spokesmen called upon to lead the discussion
were the well-known sinologist René Grousset, the neo-Thomist
philosopher Jacques Maritain, and René Guénon, who was invited
as an expert in Hinduism. *Beasts, Men and Gods* is a thrilling
account of an escape through Central Asia, in which the author
faces great hardships, meets and foils various enemies, and then
comes into contact first with shamans, and then with Mongolian
lamas, whose marvels he describes. The book caused a great sensation, especially the final chapters, in which Ossendowski recounts

legends allegedly passed on to him concerning the 'King of the World' and of his subterranean kingdom of Agarttha. Three years after this conference, Guénon published the present text, in which he develops the theme of the King of the World from the point of view of traditional metaphysics.

Guénon often uses words or expressions set off in 'scare quotes'. To avoid clutter, single quotation marks have been used throughout. As for transliterations, Guénon was more concerned with phonetic fidelity than academic usage. The system adopted here reflects the views of scholars familiar both with the languages and Guénon's writings. Brackets indicate editorial insertions, or, within citations, Guénon's additions. Wherever possible, references have been up-dated, and English editions substituted.

A translation of this work under the title *The Lord of the World* was published by Coombe Springs Press in 1983. The present translation is based on the work of Henry Fohr, edited by his son Samuel Fohr. The entire text was checked for accuracy and further revised by Marie Hansen. Editorial contributions were also made by John Champoux, John Ahmed Herlihy, William Quinn, and Mark Mancuso. A special debt of thanks is owed to Cecil Bethell, who revised and proofread the text at several stages and provided the index. Cover design by Michael Buchino and Gray Henry, based on a drawing of the Green Man, known to Islam as 'al-Khidr', by Guénon's friend and collaborator Ananda K. Coomaraswamy.

THE WORKS
OF RENÉ GUÉNON

1

WESTERN IDEAS
ABOUT *AGARTTHA*

SAINT-YVES D'ALVEYDRE's posthumous work *Mission de l'Inde*, first published in 1910,[1] contains a description of a mysterious initiatic center called Agarttha, and many readers have no doubt assumed that this was just an imaginary tale, a sort of fiction, with no basis in reality. If taken literally, it does in fact contain some improbable accounts that could justify such an appraisal, at least for those accustomed to seeing only external appearances, and Saint-Yves doubtless had good reasons for not publishing the book, which was written long ago but never brought to completion. Moreover, until the appearance of this book there had hardly been any mention in Europe of Agarttha and its leader the *Brahmātmā*, except by the rather superficial writer Louis Jacolliot [1837–1890], whose authority one cannot possibly invoke. In our opinion Jacolliot had actually heard of these things while in India, but created his own fantasy about them, as he did with everything else.[2] However,

---

1. Second edition, 1949.

2. *Les Fils de Dieu* [Paris: C. Marpon et E. Flammarion, 1882], pp 236, 213–67, 272; *Le Spiritisme dans le monde: L'initiation et les sciences occultes dans l'Inde et chez tous les peuples de l'antique* [Paris: Lacroix et Cie, 1879], pp 27–8. [The second of these two books was translated into English under the title *Occult Science in India and among the Ancients: with an Account of their Mystic Initiations and the History of Spiritualism* (Kila, MT: Kessinger Pub. Co., 1994), orig. pub. in 1875; and another title, *Bible dans l'Inde*, was translated as *The Bible in India: Hindoo Origin of Hebrew and Christian Revelation* (Santa Fe, NM: Sun Pub. Co., 1992), orig. pub. in 1869; one other English source is *Mystics & Magicians of India: An Anthology* (Calcutta: Susil Gupta, 1953). ED.]

in 1924 a book entitled *Beasts, Men and Gods* appeared unexpect-
edly on the scene, in which the author, Ferdinand Ossendowski,
relates the incidents of a most eventful journey he made across
Central Asia in the years 1920 and 1921, including, especially in its
latter part, accounts almost identical with those given by Saint-
Yves; and we believe that the sensation aroused by this book at last
furnishes a favorable opportunity to break the silence on the question of Agarttha.

Naturally, hostile and sceptical critics did not fail to accuse
Ossendowski of simply plagiarizing Saint-Yves, supporting their
allegation by pointing out all the concordant passages in the two
books; and in fact there are a good number that show a rather
astonishing similarity, even to points of detail. First of all, in one of
his most improbable passages, Saint-Yves asserts the existence of a
subterranean world with branches everywhere—under continents
and even under the oceans—by means of which communications
are invisibly established between all the regions of the earth; moreover, Ossendowski does not affirm this on his own authority, even
declaring that he does not know what to think of it, but attributes it
rather to reports received from people he met in the course of his
journey. On a more particular point, there is also a passage in which
the 'King of the World' is depicted in front of his predecessor's tomb
and where the question is raised concerning the origin of the gypsies,[3] who, among others, are said to have lived originally in Agarttha. Saint-Yves writes that there are moments during the subterranean celebration of the 'cosmic mysteries' when travelers upon
the desert stop motionless and even the animals are silent; and
Ossendowski has assured us that he himself was present at such a
moment of universal contemplation.[4] But most important of all, by
a strange coincidence both writers tell the story of an island now

3. We should say in this connection that the existence of peoples 'in tribulation',
of whom the gypsies are one of the most striking examples, is truly something very
mysterious and well worth close examination.

4. Arturo Reghini called our attention to the fact that this could have some relation to the *timor panicus* of the ancients, a connection that does indeed seem quite
likely.

vanished where extraordinary men and beasts once lived; at this point Saint-Yves cites the summary by Diodorus of Sicily of the journey of Iambulus, whereas Ossendowski describes the journey of an ancient Buddhist from Nepal; but their accounts hardly differ, so that if two versions from such widely divergent sources really do exist it would be interesting to acquire them and compare them carefully.

Although we have pointed to these similarities, it should be emphasized that we are in no way convinced that there was indeed plagiarism; and we do not in any case intend to enter into a discussion of only limited interest. We know through other sources, independent of the evidence offered by Ossendowski himself, that stories of this kind are current in Mongolia and throughout Central Asia, and we can immediately add that there is something similar in the traditions of nearly all peoples. Furthermore, if Ossendowski did in part copy from the *Mission de l'Inde*, it is difficult to see why he should have omitted certain passages or changed the form of certain words, writing *Agharti* in place of Agarttha, for example, which on the contrary is easily explained if he received from a Mongolian source the information that Saint-Yves obtained from a Hindu source (the latter being known to have been in contact with at least two Hindus);[5] nor is it easy to understand why he would have used the title 'King of the World' to designate the head of the initiatic hierarchy, a title that appears nowhere in Saint-Yves's work. Even if a certain amount of borrowing were admitted, the fact remains that Ossendowski sometimes says things that have no equivalent in *Mission de l'Inde* and that he certainly would not have

5. Ossendowski's adversaries wished to explain the same fact by claiming that he had at hand a Russian translation of *Mission de l'Inde*, but the existence of such a translation is more than doubtful since the heirs of Saint-Yves himself have no knowledge of it; they have also reproached Ossendowski for writing *Om* where Saint-Yves writes *Aum*; now if *Aum* is indeed the representation of the sacred monosyllable split into its constituent elements, *Om* is nevertheless a transcription that is both correct and that corresponds to the actual pronunciation as it exists in India as well as in Tibet and Mongolia; this detail alone suffices to appraise the competence of such critics.

been able to invent in their entirety, all the more so as he was far more preoccupied with politics than with the pursuit of ideas or doctrines, and was so ignorant of anything touching on esoterism that he was manifestly incapable of grasping the true import of such things. For example, he tells the story of the 'black stone' that had originally been sent by the 'King of the World' to the Dalai Lama, and subsequently transported to Urga in Mongolia, where it disappeared approximately one hundred years ago;[6] now, in many traditions 'black stones' play an important role, from that played by the symbol of Cybele to that of the stone enshrined in the *Kaaba* at Mecca.[7] Here is another example: the *Bogdo-Khan* or 'Living Buddha', who resides at Urga, preserves, among other precious items, the ring of Genghis Khan, on which is engraved a *swastika*, and a copper plaque bearing the seal of the 'King of the World'; it seems that Ossendowski managed to see only the first of these two objects, but, if this is so, would it not then have been extremely difficult for him to conjure the other from his imagination, and would it not have been more natural for him to describe a plaque of *gold?*

These preliminary observations must suffice, for we wish to remain apart from any polemics or questions of personalities; we have only cited Ossendowski and Saint-Yves as a point of departure for considerations that have nothing to do with what one might think of either of them, and whose importance exceeds their individualities, as well as our own, which in this domain should no longer count. Nor do we propose a more or less vain 'textual

---

6. Ossendowski, who does not know that the stone is a meteorite, tries to explain certain phenomena, such as the appearance of writing on its surface, by supposing that it was a kind of slate.

7. A curious connection could also be made with the *lapsit exillis*, a stone fallen from heaven, on which inscriptions also appear under certain circumstances, and which is identified with the Grail in the account of Wolfram von Eschenbach. What makes it still more unusual is that, according to this same account, the Grail was finally transported to the 'Kingdom of Prester John', which some have wished to identify precisely with Mongolia, despite the fact that no geographical localization can be accepted literally in this case (cf. *The Esoterism of Dante*, chap. 4).

criticism', but rather a presentation of some information that, to our knowledge, has been unavailable until now, and that might help in some measure to elucidate what Ossendowski calls the 'mystery of mysteries'.[8]

8. We were quite surprised to learn recently that certain people claim the present book as a 'testimony' in favor of a personage whose very existence was entirely unknown to us at the time it was written; we strenuously deny such assertions, from whatever quarter they may come, for we are concerned exclusively with setting forth information pertaining to traditional symbolism, which has absolutely nothing to do with any 'personifications' whatsoever.

2

ROYALTY
AND PONTIFICATE

THE title 'King of the World', taken in its highest, most complete, and at the same time most rigorous sense, applies properly to *Manu*, the primordial and universal legislator, whose name is found in diverse forms among a great many ancient peoples; in this regard, let us recall only *Mina*, or *Menes*, of the Egyptians, *Menw* of the Celts, and *Minos* of the Greeks.[1] This name moreover does not designate a more or less legendary historical personage, but rather a principle, a cosmic Intelligence that reflects pure spiritual light and formulates the Law (*Dharma*) appropriate to the conditions of our world and of our cycle of existence; and at the same time it is the archetype of man, considered particularly insofar as he is a thinking being (in Sanskrit, *mānava*).

Moreover, it is important to emphasize that this principle can be manifested through a spiritual center existing in the terrestrial world by an organization charged with preserving intact the deposit of sacred tradition, which is of 'non-human' origin (*apaurusheya*), through which primordial Wisdom is handed down across the ages to those capable of receiving it. The head of such an organization, representing in a way *Manu* himself, can legitimately bear his title and attributes; and what is more, the degree of knowledge he must have attained to exercise his function enables him to truly identify

---

1. Among the Greeks, *Minos* was at the same time both legislator of the living and judge of the dead; in the Hindu tradition these two functions belong respectively to *Manu* and *Yama*, who are moreover represented as twin brothers, which indicates the splitting into two of a single principle envisaged under two different aspects.

himself with the principle of which he is the human expression, as it were, and before which his individuality disappears. Such is indeed the case of Agarttha, if, as Saint-Yves maintains, this center has taken over the heritage of the ancient 'solar dynasty' (*Sūrya-van-sha*), which formerly resided at Ayodhyā,[2] and which traced its origin back to *Vaivasvata*, the *Manu* of the present cycle.

Nevertheless, as we have said, Saint-Yves does not in fact envisage the supreme head of Agarttha as the 'King of the World', but presents him as 'Sovereign Pontiff', whom moreover he places at the head of a 'Brahmanic church', a designation that proceeds from a rather too Westernized conception.[3] This last reservation apart, what he says in this regard complements what Ossendowski says, both writers having seen only that aspect corresponding to their own tendencies and dominant preoccupations, for in truth it is here a matter of a double power, at once sacerdotal and royal. The 'pontific' character, in the proper sense of this word, belongs most truly and par excellence to the head of the initiatic hierarchy, and this calls for an explanation: *Pontifex* literally means 'builder of bridges', and by its origin this Roman title is as it were 'masonic'; but symbolically it is that which fulfills the function of mediator, establishing communication between this world and the higher worlds.[4] In this respect, the rainbow or 'celestial bridge' is a natural symbol for the pontificate and

2. Envisaged symbolically, this seat of the 'solar dynasty' can be likened to the 'Solar Citadel' of the Rosicrucians, and doubtless also to Campanella's 'City of the Sun'.

3. This expression 'Brahmanic church' has as a matter of fact never been used in India, except by the heterodox and entirely modern sect of the *Brahma-Samāj*, which arose at the beginning of the nineteenth century under European, and particularly Protestant, influences, soon to be splintered into a multitude of rival branches, which today have almost completely disappeared. It is curious to note that one of the founders of this sect was the grandfather of the poet Rabindranath Tagore.

4. Saint Bernard said that 'the pontiff, as indicated by the etymology of this name, is a sort of bridge between God and man' (*Tractatus de Moribus et Officio Episcoporum*, III, 9).

In India there is a term peculiar to the Jains that is the strict equivalent of the Latin *pontifex*: it is the word *Tīrthankara*, literally 'he who makes a ford or crossing', the crossing in question being the way of Deliverance (*Moksha*). The *Tīrthankaras* number twenty-four, as do the ancients of the Apocalypse, who moreover also constitute a pontifical college.

all traditions give it perfectly concordant meanings; thus among the Hebrews it is the sign of God's covenant with his people; in China it is the sign of the union of Heaven and Earth; in Greece it represents *Iris*, 'the messenger of the gods'; and almost everywhere—among the Scandinavians as well as the Persians and Arabs, in Central Africa, and even among certain peoples of North America—it is the bridge that links the sensible world to the suprasensible.

Among the Romans, on the other hand, this union of sacerdotal and royal power was represented by a certain aspect of the extremely complex and multivalent symbolism of *Janus*, whose gold and silver keys represented, in this connection, the two corresponding initiations.[5] In Hindu terms, it is a matter of the ways of the Brahmin and the Kshatriya respectively; but at the summit of the hierarchy there is a common principle from which both draw their respective attributes, and which is therefore beyond these distinctions since this principle is the source of all legitimate authority, in whatever domain it is exercised; and the initiates of Agarttha are *ativarna*, that is to say, 'beyond caste'.[6]

In the Middle Ages there was an expression in which these two complementary aspects of authority were joined in an interesting way. At that time frequent mention was made of a mysterious region called the 'Kingdom of Prester John'.[7] Now this was at a time when what could be called the 'outer covering' of the initiatic center

5. From another point of view these keys are respectively those of the 'greater mysteries' and the 'lesser mysteries'. In certain representations of *Janus*, the two powers are also symbolized by a key and a scepter.

6. It is to be noted in this connection that the social organization of the Western Middle Ages seems to have been modeled in principle on the institution of castes: the clergy corresponded to the Brahmins, the nobility to the Kshatriyas, the third estate to the Vaishyas, and the serfs to the Shūdras.

7. The matter of Prester John arises particularly around the time of Saint Louis, in connection with the travels of Carpin and de Rubruquis. What complicates matters is that, according to certain accounts, there were as many as four personages who bore this title: in Tibet (or in the Pamir), in Mongolia, in India, and in Ethiopia (this last word having in any case a very vague meaning); but it is likely a matter of different representatives of the same power. It is also said that Genghis Khan wanted to attack the kingdom of Prester John, but that the latter repulsed him by unleashing thunderbolts against his armies. And finally, since the time of the Muslim invasions Prester John seems no longer to have manifested himself, though he is perhaps outwardly represented by the Dalai Lama.

in question was formed in large part by Nestorians (or those who were so called, rightly or wrongly), and by Sabaeans,[8] who referred to themselves as the *Mendayyeh de Yahia*, that is, 'disciples of John'. In this connection, one is immediately prompted to remark that it is curious that many Eastern organizations, which were rigidly closed communities—from the Ismāʿīlīs, or the disciples of the 'Old Man of the Mountain', to the Druses of Lebanon—have without exception taken the same title 'Guardians of the Holy Land' as did the Western Orders of Chivalry; what follows will no doubt clarify just what this means. It seems that Saint-Yves found the right expression, perhaps more so than he himself knew, when he spoke of the 'Templars of Agarttha'. And, lest one be astonished at the expression 'outer covering' that we have just employed, we will add that it must be understood that the chivalric initiation was essentially an initiation of the Kshatriyas; and this explains, among other things, the preponderant role played there by the symbolism of Love.[9]

However that may be, the idea of one individual who is both priest and king is not current in the contemporary West, although it is found at the very origins of Christianity, where it is represented in a striking way by the 'Magi-kings'; but already by the Middle Ages, at least to outer appearances, the supreme power had become divided between the papacy and the empire.[10] Such a separation can be considered the mark of an organization that is incomplete at its summit, so to speak, since there we do not find the common principle from which the two powers regularly proceed and on which they depend, the true supreme power having therefore to be sought elsewhere. In the East, on the contrary, the maintenance of such a

---

8. In Central Asia, and particularly in the region of Turkestan, Nestorian crosses have been found that are identical in form to the crosses of chivalry, some of which moreover bear at their center the figure of the *swastika*. On the other hand, it is noteworthy that the Nestorians, whose connections with Lamaism seem incontestable, had an important though enigmatic influence on the beginnings of Islam. The Sabaeans for their part exerted a great influence on the Arab world at the time of the Caliphs of Baghdad; and it is also said that it was among them that the last of the Neoplatonists found refuge after their sojourn in Persia.

9. We have already called attention to this in our study *The Esoterism of Dante*.

10. In ancient Rome, on the contrary, the emperor was also *Pontifex Maximus*. The Islamic theory of the Caliphate also unites the two powers, at least to a certain extent, as does the Far-Eastern notion of the *Wang* (see *The Great Triad*, chap. 17).

separation at the very summit of the hierarchy is rather exceptional, and it is only in certain Buddhist conceptions that one encounters something of the kind. Here we allude to the incompatibility affirmed between the function of *Buddha* and that of *Chakravartī*, or the 'Universal Monarch',[11] between which, it is said, Shākyamuni had to choose at a certain point.

It is worth adding also that the term *Chakravartī*, far from being particularly Buddhist, applies very well to the function of *Manu* or of his representatives, following the Hindu tradition; literally, it means 'he who makes the wheel turn', which is to say he who, placed at the center of all things, directs their movement without himself participating therein, or, according to Aristotle's expression, he who is the 'unmoved mover'.[12]

We particularly wish to emphasize that, since the world rotates around it, the center in question is the fixed point that all traditions refer to symbolically as the 'Pole', generally represented by a wheel among the Celts and Chaldeans as well as the Hindus.[13] Such is the true significance of the *swastika*, a symbol found everywhere, from the Far East to the Far West, and which is essentially the 'sign of the Pole';[14] and this is no doubt the first time in modern Europe that its real meaning is being made known. Indeed, contemporary scholars have employed all manner of fantastic theories in their vain efforts to explain this symbol, the majority of them, obsessed by a sort of fixed idea, having been intent on seeing here, as almost everywhere

11. We have noted elsewhere the analogy between the conception of the *Chakravartī* and Dante's idea of the Empire; his treatise *De Monarchia* should be mentioned in this connection.

12. In a quite comparable sense Chinese tradition uses the expression 'Invariable Middle'; and it should be noted also that according to Masonic symbolism the Masters gather in the 'Middle Room'.

13. The Celtic symbol of the wheel was retained in the Middle Ages. Numerous examples of it are to be found in Romanesque churches, and the rose-window found in Gothic architecture seems to have derived from it, for there is a certain relationship between the wheel and the emblematic flowers, such as the rose in the West and the lotus in the East.

14. This same sign was not unknown to Christian Hermeticism. In the ancient Carmelite monastery in Loudun we have seen some very curious symbols, most likely dating from the second half of the fifteenth century, in which the *swastika*,

else, an exclusively 'solar' symbol, whereas, if it has occasionally become such, this could only have been by accident, as a result of some distortion.[15] Others have come nearer the truth when they see in the *swastika* a symbol of movement, although this interpretation, without being false, is quite insufficient, for it is not a question of just any kind of movement, but of rotational movement around a center or immutable axis; and it is this fixed point, we repeat, that constitutes the essential element to which the symbol in question is directly related.[16]

From what we have just said, it is already clear that the 'King of the World' must have a function that is essentially organizational and regulatory (it being not without reason, let us add, that this latter word possesses the same root as *rex* and *regere*), a function that can be summed up in words such as 'equilibrium' or 'harmony', which is rendered precisely by the Sanskrit term *Dharma*,[17] by which we understand the reflection in the manifested world of the immutability of the supreme Principle. And in the same way, it is understandable why the fundamental attributes of the 'King of the

together with the sign ⋈ (which we shall discuss later), occupies one of the most important positions. And it is noteworthy that the Carmelites, who came from the East, link the founding of their order to Elias and to Pythagoras (just as the Masons for their part link their origins to both Solomon and Pythagoras, which constitutes a rather remarkable parallel), and that elsewhere some people even claim that in the Middle Ages they had an initiation very close to that of the Templars and also to that of the monks of the Order of Mercy; it is known that this latter Order gave its name to a certain grade of Scottish Masonry, about which we have written at some length in *The Esoterism of Dante*.

15. The same remark applies notably to the wheel, the true significance of which has just been indicated.

16. We will only cite, for the record, the even more fanciful opinion that makes of the *swastika* a diagram of a primitive instrument intended for the production of fire; if this symbol does sometimes have a certain connection with fire (being in particular an emblem of *Agni*), this is for quite other reasons.

17. The root *dhri* expresses essentially the idea of stability; the form *dhru*, which has the same meaning, is the root of *Dhruva*, the Sanskrit name for the Pole, which some connect with the Greek name for the oak, *drus*; in Latin, moreover, the same word *robur* signifies the oak as well as strength or firmness. Among the Druids (whose name should perhaps be read *dru-vid*, uniting strength and wisdom), and also at Dodona, the oak represented the 'World Tree', symbol of the fixed axis that joins the poles.

World' are 'Justice' and 'Peace', which are only the special forms of this equilibrium and harmony in the 'world of man' (*mānavaloka*).[18] Here again is a point of the greatest importance, which we note not only because of its general significance, but for the benefit of those who allow themselves to succumb to certain chimerical fears, of which Ossendowski's book itself contains a sort of echo in its closing lines.

18. Recall here the biblical texts in which Justice and Peace are closely joined: *Justitiae et Pax osculatae sunt* (Ps. 84:11), *Pax opus Justiti*, etc.

3

SHEKINAH
AND METATRON

CERTAIN TIMID MINDS, whose understanding is strangely limited by preconceived notions, have been frightened by the title 'King of the World', which they immediately associate with the *Princeps huius mundi* ['Prince of this world'] of the Gospels. It goes without saying that such an assimilation is wholly erroneous and lacks any foundation. The issue can be laid to rest simply by observing that the title 'King of the World', in Hebrew and in Arabic, is readily applied to God himself;[1] and this gives us occasion for some interesting observations concerning the theories of 'celestial intermediaries' in the Hebrew Kabbalah, theories that have moreover a direct bearing on the principal subject of this study.

The 'celestial intermediaries' in question are the *Shekinah* and *Metatron*, the former denoting in the most general sense the 'real presence' of the Divinity. The scriptures that make special mention of this presence are above all those concerned with the establishment of a spiritual center, such as the construction of the Tabernacle and the building of the Temples of Solomon and of Zorobabel. Such a center, constituted in rigorously defined conditions, must be a place of divine manifestation, which is always represented as 'Light';

---

1. Besides, there is a great difference of meaning between 'the World' and 'this world', so much so that in certain languages two entirely distinct terms are used to designate them: thus, in Arabic 'the World' is *al-'ālam*, while 'this world' is *ad-dunyā*.

and it is curious to note that the expression 'a well-illuminated and ordered place', still retained by the Masons, seems to be a vestige of the ancient sacerdotal science that oversaw the construction of the temples, and that furthermore was not peculiar to the Jews, a point we shall take up later. Here we need not enter into the theory of 'spiritual influences' (a better translation of the Hebrew *berakoth* than the usual 'blessings', more particularly as it keeps the sense that the Arabic *barakah* has retained); but even limiting ourselves to this one point of view, it is still possible to explain Elias Levita's statement, as quoted by Vulliaud in his *La Kabbale juive*, that 'the masters of the Kabbalah hold great secrets on this subject.'

The *Shekinah* is presented under a number of aspects, among which two are primary, the one inward and the other outward; moreover, in the Christian tradition there is an expression that indicates these two aspects in the clearest possible way: *Gloria in excelsis Deo, et in terra Pax hominibus bonae voluntatis.* The words *Gloria* and *Pax* refer respectively to the inward aspect with respect to its relation to the principle, and the outer aspect with respect to its relation to the manifested world; and in considering these words it is immediately clear why they are spoken by the angels (*Malakim*) to announce the birth of God 'with us', or 'in us' (*Emmanuel*). Regarding the first aspect, one could also recall the theories of the theologians on 'the light of glory' in and by which the beatific vision operates (*in excelsis*); and as to the second, we find here again the 'Peace' to which we just alluded, and which, in its esoteric sense, is everywhere indicated as one of the fundamental attributes of the spiritual centers established in this world (*in terra*). Furthermore, the Arabic term *Sakīnah*, obviously identical to the Hebrew *Shekinah*, translates as 'Great Peace', which is an exact equivalent of the *Pax Profunda* of the Brotherhood of the Rose-Cross; and on this basis one could doubtless explain what the latter meant by the 'Temple of the Holy Spirit', just as one could also give a precise interpretation to the numerous Gospel texts in which 'Peace'[2] is

---

2. The Gospels themselves quite explicitly declare moreover that what is in question is not peace as understood by the profane world (John 14:27).

mentioned, all the more so as 'the secret tradition concerning the *Shekinah* must have some connection with the light of the Messiah.' Was it only coincidental that in making this last point, Vulliaud said that it concerns the tradition 'reserved for those who pursue the path leading to *Pardes*,' that is to say, as will be seen later on, to the supreme spiritual center?[3]

This leads to a related point: Vulliaud speaks subsequently of a 'mystery related to the Jubilee',[4] which in turn relates in one sense to the idea of 'Peace', and in this connection he cites the text of the *Zohar* (iii, 52, b): 'The river that flows out of Eden bears the name *Iobel*,' as well as that of Jeremiah (17:8): 'It is like a tree planted by water, that sends out its roots by the stream'; from which it follows that 'the central idea of the Jubilee is the return of all things to their primordial state.' It is clear that it is this return to the 'primordial state' envisaged by all traditions, a point upon which we had occasion to dwell in our book *The Esoterism of Dante*; and if we add that 'the return of all things to their primordial state will herald the messianic era,' those who have read the book may then recall what it said about the relationship between the 'Terrestrial Paradise' and the 'Celestial Jerusalem'. In truth, moreover, what is involved here in various phases of cyclical manifestation is always *Pardes*, the center of this world, which the traditional symbolism of all peoples likens to the heart, the center of the being and the 'divine residence' (*Brahma-pura* in Hindu doctrine); the Tabernacle, which is made in its image, is therefore called in Hebrew *mishkan*, or 'dwelling of God', a word having the same root as *Shekinah*.

From another point of view the *Shekinah* is the synthesis of the *Sephiroth*; now in the sephirothic tree the 'right-hand column' is the side of Mercy and the 'left-hand column' is that of Rigor;[5] we should therefore find both of these aspects in the *Shekinah*, and we

3. *La Kabbale juive*, vi, p503.
4. Ibid., i, pp 506–7.
5. A comparable symbolism is expressed by the medieval figure of the 'tree of the living and the dead', which moreover has an obvious connection with the idea of 'spiritual posterity'; note also that the sephirothic tree is considered to be identical to the 'Tree of Life'.

note immediately, in connection with what was said before, that, in certain respects at least, Rigor is identified with Justice, and Mercy with Peace.[6] 'If man sins and strays from the *Shekinah*, he falls under the jurisdiction of the powers (*Sārim*) that derive from Rigor,'[7] and then the *Shekinah* is called the 'hand of rigor', which immediately calls to mind the well-known symbol of the 'hand of justice'; but if, on the contrary, 'a man approaches the *Shekinah*, he will be liberated,' and then the *Shekinah* is the 'right hand' of God, which is to say that the 'hand of justice' becomes the 'hand of blessing'.[8] These are the mysteries of the 'House of Justice' (*Beith-Din*), which is yet another designation of the supreme spiritual center;[9] and it is scarcely necessary to point out that the two sides under discussion are identical to those into which the elect and the damned are separated in Christian representations of the 'Last Judgement'. One could equally well establish a connection with the two paths which the Pythagoreans symbolized by the letter 'Y' (represented exoterically as Virtue and Vice in the myth of Hercules) as well as with the two doors, celestial and infernal, which the Romans associated with the symbolism of *Janus*, and also with the two cyclical phases,[10] ascending and descending, which the Hindus similarly

6. According to the *Talmud*, God has two seats, that of Justice and that of Mercy, these two seats corresponding also to the 'throne' and to the 'chair' of Islamic tradition. The latter, in addition, divide the divine names (the *ṣifātiyah*, that is, those that properly speaking express the so-called attributes of *Allah*) into 'names of majesty' (*jalāliya*) and 'names of beauty' (*jamāliya*), which again corresponds to a distinction of the same order.

7. *La Kabbale juive*, I, p 507.

8. According to Saint Augustine and certain other Fathers of the Church, the right hand similarly represents Mercy or Goodness, whereas the left hand, of God especially, is the symbol of Justice. The 'hand of justice' is one of the usual attributes of royalty; the 'hand of blessing' is a sign of sacerdotal authority and has sometimes been taken as a symbol of Christ. This figure of the 'hand of blessing' is found on certain Gallic coins, as is also the *swastika*, sometimes with curved arms.

9. This center, or any one of those that are constituted in its image, can be described symbolically as both a temple (the sacerdotal aspect, corresponding to Peace) and a palace or tribunal (the royal aspect, corresponding to Justice).

10. We have here the two halves of the zodiacal circle, which is frequently represented on the portals of medieval churches in a manner clearly giving them the same significance.

associated with the symbolism of Ganesha.[11] Finally, it is easy to understand from all this what is truly meant by such expressions as 'right intention' (to which we shall return later) and 'good will',[12] when one leaves aside all those external interpretations, moral and philosophical, to which they have given rise from the Stoics through Kant.

'The Kabbalah gives to the *Shekinah* a consort who bears names identical with her own and consequently possesses the same characteristics',[13] and who naturally also possesses as many different aspects as the *Shekinah* herself. His name is *Metatron*, which is numerically equivalent to that of *Shaddaï*,[14] the 'All-Powerful' (said to be the name of the God of Abraham). The etymology of the word *Metatron* is most obscure; among the many hypotheses that have been advanced, one of the most interesting is its derivation from the Chaldean *Mitra*, which means 'rain', and which by its root is also sometimes related to 'light'. Even if this is so, the similarity with the Hindu and Zoroastrian *Mitra* does not constitute a sufficient reason to conclude that it represents a Jewish borrowing from foreign doctrines, for it is not in this wholly external manner that the relationship existing between the different traditions should be envisaged; and we shall say the same concerning the role attributed to rain in almost all traditions, insofar as it is a symbol of the descent of 'spiritual influences' from Heaven to Earth. Moreover, it is worth noting in this connection that the Hebraic doctrine speaks of a 'dew of light' emanating from the 'Tree of Life', by which the resurrection of the dead is to be effected, as well as of an 'effusion of dew' that represents the celestial influence communicating itself to all the worlds, which is singularly reminiscent of alchemical and Rosicrucian symbolism.

11. All the symbols enumerated would need to be explained at length, something we hope to do in a future work. [See *Symbols of Sacred Science.* Ed.]

12. 'Pax hominibus *bonae voluntatis*'; and those familiar with the various symbols we have just mentioned will see that it is not without reason that Christmas coincides with the time of the winter solstice.

13. *La Kabbale juive*, I, pp 497–8.

14. The number of each of these two names, obtained by adding the values of the Hebrew letters of which they are composed, is 314.

'The term *Metatron* conveys the multiple meanings of guardian, lord, messenger, mediator'; he is the 'author of theophanies in the world of the senses';[15] he is the 'Angel of the Face', and also the 'Prince of the World' *(Sār ha-ōlam)*, this last designation indicating that we have not strayed from our subject. Employing the traditional symbolism that has already been explained, we readily say that just as the head of the initiatic hierarchy is the 'terrestrial Pole', so *Metatron* is the 'celestial Pole'; the latter has his reflection in the former, with whom he stands in direct relation through the 'World Axis'. 'His name is *Mikaël*, the Great Priest who is both holocaust and oblation before God. And everything the Israelites do on earth is accomplished according to the archetypes of events in the celestial world. The Great Pontiff here below represents *Mikaël*, prince of Mercy. . . . Every scriptural passage that tells of an appearance of *Mikaël* is also concerned with the glory of the *Shekinah*.'[16] What is said here of the Israelites could equally well be said of all peoples possessing a genuinely orthodox tradition, and all the more so of the representatives of the primordial tradition, from which all the other traditions derive, and to which they are subordinate, all this in accord with the symbolism of the 'Holy Land', an image of the celestial world, to which we have already alluded. Moreover, according to what was said above, *Metatron* possesses not only the aspect of Mercy but also that of Justice; he is not only the 'Great Priest' *(Kohen ha-gadol)* but also the 'Great Prince' *(Sār ha-gadol)* and 'commander of the celestial hosts', which is to say that in him lies both the principle of the royal power, and that of the sacerdotal or pontifical power to which properly corresponds the function of 'mediator'. And we should add that *Melek*, 'king', and *Malak*, 'angel' or 'messenger', are really two forms of one and the same word; and in addition, *Malaki*, 'my messenger' (that is, the messenger of God, or the 'angel in whom God dwells', *Malak ha-Elohim*), is an anagram of *Mikaël*.[17]

---

15. *La Kabbale juive*, I, pp 492 and 499.

16. Ibid., I, pp 500–1.

17. This last remark naturally brings to mind the words *Benedictus qui venit in nomine Domini* ['Blessed is he who comes in the name of the Lord'], which are applied to Christ, whom the *Shepherd of Hermas* assimilates precisely to *Mikaël* in a

It is proper to add that if *Mikaël* is identified with *Metatron*, as we have just seen, he nevertheless represents only one aspect of him; besides the luminous face, there is a dark face represented by *Samaël*, who is called also *Sār ha-ōlam*, thereby bringing us back to the point of departure in this discussion. It is in fact this latter aspect, and it alone, that symbolizes in an inferior sense the 'spirit of this world', the *Princeps huius mundi* referred to in the Gospels; and its connection with *Metatron*, of whom it is the shadow, so to speak, justifies the use of the one title in a twofold sense, at the same time making clear why the apocalyptic number 666, the 'number of the Beast', is also a solar number.[18] According to Saint Hippolytus, 'the Messiah and the Antichrist both have the lion for their emblem,'[19] and it, too, is a solar symbol; and the same could be said of the serpent[20] and of many other symbols. From a kabbalistic point of view it is again the two opposing faces of *Metatron* that are here in question; at this point we need not enter into the theories that could be formulated in a general way on this double meaning of symbols, but will only note that the confusion between the luminous and dark aspects is what properly constitutes 'satanism', and that it is precisely this confusion which allows some, no doubt unintentionally and through simple ignorance (an excuse, but not a justification), to believe that they have uncovered an infernal significance in the title 'King of the World'.[21]

way that may seem rather strange, but that should not surprise those who understand the connection between the Messiah and the *Shekinah*. Christ is also called 'the Prince of Peace', and he is at the same time the 'Judge of the living and the dead'.

18. This number is formed notably by the name of *Sorath*, demon of the sun, and opposed as such to the angel *Mikaël*; we will later see a further significance to this number.

19. Cited by Vulliaud, *La Kabbale juive*, ii, p373.

20. The two opposing aspects are figured notably by the two serpents of the caduceus; in Christian iconography they are reunited in the 'amphisbaena', the two-headed serpent, one of which represents Christ and the other satan.

21. Let us point out further that the 'Globe of the World', insignia of imperial power or of universal monarchy, is frequently placed in the hand of Christ, which shows moreover that it is the emblem of spiritual authority as well as of temporal power.

4

THE THREE
SUPREME FUNCTIONS

ACCORDING TO SAINT-YVES, the supreme head of Agarttha bears the title of *Brahātmā* (it would be more correct to say *Brahmātmā*) or 'support of souls in the Spirit of God'; his two adjuncts are the *Mahātmā*, 'representative of the universal Soul', and the *Mahānga*, 'symbol of the entire material organization of the Cosmos'.[1] These comprise the hierarchic division represented in Western doctrines by the ternary of 'spirit', 'soul', and 'body', applied here according to the analogy of the macrocosm and the microcosm. It is important to note that these terms, in Sanskrit, properly denote principles, and that they cannot be applied to human beings except insofar as they represent these principles, so that, even in such cases, they are attached essentially to functions and not to individualities. According to Ossendowski, the *Mahātmā* 'knows the events of the future' and the *Mahānga* 'directs the course of those events'; as for the *Brahātmā*, he is able to 'speak to God face to face',[2] and it is easy to understand what this means if one remembers that he occupies the central point from which direct communication is established between the terrestrial world and the superior states, and, through these latter, with the supreme Principle.[3] Besides, if the term 'King of the World' were interpreted in a restricted sense and solely in relation to the terrestrial world, it would prove inadequate; it would

1. Ossendowski writes *Brahytma*, *Mahytma*, and *Mahynga*.
2. We have seen above that *Metatron* is 'the Angel of the Face'.
3. According to Far-Eastern tradition, the 'Invariable Middle' is the point at which the 'Activity of Heaven' is manifested.

be more accurate, in certain respects, to designate *Brahātmā* as 'Lord of the three worlds',[4] for in every true hierarchy he who possesses the superior degree thereby also possesses at the same time all the subordinate degrees, and as we shall explain further on, these 'three worlds' (which constitute the *Tribhuvana* of Hindu tradition) are the domains corresponding respectively to the three functions we are about to specify.

'As he comes forth from the temple,' writes Ossendowski, 'the King of the World radiates Divine Light.'[5] The Hebrew Bible reports exactly the same of Moses when he came down from Mount Sinai,[6] and in this connection it is worth noting that the Islamic tradition regards Moses as the 'Pole' (*al-Quṭb*) of his age; besides, was it not for this reason that, according to the Kabbalah, he was instructed by *Metatron* himself? It is important here again to distinguish between the principal spiritual center of our world and the secondary centers subordinate to it that represent it only in relation to particular traditions, adapted more particularly to specific peoples. Without wishing to belabor the point, we should nonetheless note that the function of 'legislator' (in Arabic, *rasūl*) belonging to Moses necessarily supposes a delegation of the power designated by the name *Manu*; moreover, one of the meanings implicit in this name indicates precisely the reflection of Divine Light.

> The King of the World [said a Lama to Ossendowski] is in contact with the thoughts of all the men who influence the lot and life of all humankind. . . . He realizes all their thoughts and plans. If these be pleasing before God, the King of the World will

4. We would ask those who might be surprised at such an expression whether they have ever reflected upon the significance of the *triregnum*, the three-crowned tiara, which is, together with the keys, one of the principal insignia of the papacy.

5. Ferdinand Ossendowski, *Beasts, Men and Gods* (New York: E.P. Dutton & Company, 1923), p309.

6. It is also said that at that time Moses had to cover his face with a veil to speak to the people, who could not bear the brilliance (Exodus 24:29–35), which indicates symbolically the necessity of an exoteric adaptation for the multitude. Let us recall in this connection the double significance of the word 'reveal', which can mean 'draw aside the veil', but also 'cover again with a veil'; it is thus that the word manifests and veils, at one and the same time, the thought that it expresses.

invisibly help them; if they are unpleasant in the sight of God, the King will bring them to destruction. This power is given to Agharti by the mysterious science of *Om*, with which we begin all our prayers.[7]

There immediately follows a sentence that will greatly astonish those who have only a vague idea of the significance of this sacred monosyllable: '*Om* is the name of an ancient Holyman, the first Goro [Ossendowski writes *goro* for *guru*], who lived three hundred thousand years ago.'[8] This sentence would be completely unintelligible were it not borne in mind that the age in question, which moreover seems indicated rather vaguely, is very much anterior to the era of the present *Manu*; furthermore, the *Ādi-Manu*, or first *Manu*, of our present *Kalpa* (*Vaivasvata* being the seventh) is called *Svāyambhuva*, that is to say, issue of *Svayambhū*, 'he who subsists of himself', or the 'eternal *Logos*'; but the *Logos*, or he who represents it directly, can truly be designated the first *Guru* or 'Spiritual Master', which in effect means that *Om* is another of the names of the *Logos*.[9]

Moreover, the word *Om* immediately provides a key to the hierarchical distribution of functions between *Brahātmā* and his two

7. Ossendowski, *Beasts, Men and Gods*, p309.
8. Ibid.
9. Somewhat surprisingly, this name is also found in ancient Christian symbolism, where, among the signs that served to represent Christ, we encounter one that was later considered an abbreviation of *Ave Maria*, but which was originally an equivalent of the sign that unites the first and last letters of the Greek alphabet, *alpha* and *omega*, to signify that the Word is the beginning and the end of all things; it is in reality even more complete, for it signifies the beginning, the middle, and the end. This sign, ⋈, breaks down in fact into AVM, that is, the three Latin letters that correspond exactly to the three constituent elements of the monosyllable *om* (the vowel *o* in Sanskrit being formed by the union of *a* and *u*). The association of this sign *Aum* and the *swastika*, both taken as symbols of Christ, seems to us particularly significant when seen from this point of view. It should further be noted that the form of this same sign presents two ternaries set inversely to each other, making them in certain respects an equivalent to the 'seal of Solomon'; if the latter is considered under the form ⊠, where the horizontal median line specifies the general significance of the symbol by marking the plane of reflection or 'surface of the Waters', it is evident that both figures have the same number of lines, differing only in the placement of two of them, which, horizontal in the one, becomes vertical in the other.

adjuncts, as we have already indicated. According to Hindu tradition, the three elements of this sacred monosyllable symbolize, respectively, the 'three worlds' just alluded to, the three parts of the *Tribhuvana*: Earth (*Bhū*), Atmosphere (*Bhuvas*), and the Heavens (*Swar*), which, to use a different terminology, correspond to the world of corporeal manifestation, the world of subtle or psychic manifestation, and the non-manifested principial world.[10] In ascending order, these are the domains of the *Mahānga*, the *Mahātmā*, and the *Brahātmā*, as can easily be seen by referring to the interpretation of their titles above; and it is the relationships of subordination among these different domains that justifies the previous interpretation of *Brahātmā* as 'Lord of the three worlds'.[11] 'This one is the Lord of all; this one is the Omniscient [who sees at once all effects in their cause]; this one is the inner Director of all [who resides at the center of the world and governs it from within, directing its movement without participating in it]; this one is the Source of all [legitimate power]; this one is verily the place of origin and dissolution of all beings [of the cyclical manifestation whose Law he represents].'[12] To use still another symbolism that is no less exact, we can say that the *Mahānga* represents the base of the initiatic triangle and the *Brahātmā* its summit; between these two the *Mahātmā* embodies in a certain way a mediating principle (the cosmic vitality, the *Anima Mundi* of the Hermeticists), whose action is deployed in the 'intermediate realm'. All of this is represented very

10. For a fuller treatment of the conception of the 'three worlds', the reader is referred to *The Esoterism of Dante* and *Man and His Becoming according to the Vedānta*. In the first we insisted above all on the correspondence of these worlds, which are properly speaking states of the being, with the degrees of initiation; in the second we gave in particular a complete explanation, from the purely metaphysical point of view, of the text of the *Māndūkya Upanishad*, in which the symbolism here in question is set out in full, the present discussion covering only one particular application of it.

11. In the order of universal principles, the function of *Brahātmā* refers to *Ishvara*, that of *Mahātmā* to *Hiranyagarbha*, and that of *Mahānga* to *Virāj*, from which correspondence their respective attributes may easily be deduced.

12. *Māndūkya Upanishad*, shruti 6 [in the translation of Swami Gambhirananda, *Eight Principal Upaniṣads* (Calcutta: Advaita Ashrama, 1973). Bracketed insertions are Guénon's. Ed.].

clearly by the corresponding letters of the sacred alphabet that Saint-Yves calls *vattan* and that Ossendowski calls *vattanan*, or, which amounts to the same thing, by the geometric forms (straight line, spiral, and point) to which the three *mātrās*, or elements constituting the monosyllable *Om*, can be reduced.

Let us make this even clearer: to the *Brahātmā* belongs the fullness of both the sacerdotal and the royal power, envisaged principally in a kind of undifferentiated state; the two powers are subsequently differentiated in order to be manifested, the *Mahātmā* representing more particularly the sacerdotal power, and the *Mahānga* the royal power. The distinction corresponds to that between Brahmins and Kshatriyas, although in other respects the *Mahātmā* and the *Mahānga*, being 'beyond caste', have in themselves, as does the *Brahātmā*, a character at once sacerdotal and royal. This raises a most important point that seems never to have been explained satisfactorily: it has already been mentioned that the two powers were united in the 'Magi-Kings' of the Gospels; we can now say that in reality these mysterious personages represent nothing other than the three heads of Agarttha.[13] The *Mahānga* offers gold to Christ and hails him as 'King'; the *Mahātmā* offers incense and hails him as 'Priest'; and finally the *Brahātmā*, hailing him as 'Prophet', or Spiritual Master par excellence, offers myrrh (the balm of incorruptibility, symbol of *Amrita*).[14] The homage rendered in this way to the new-born Christ by the authentic representatives of the primordial tradition in the three worlds which are their respective domains, is at the same time, we should clearly note, the assurance of the perfect orthodoxy of Christianity in this respect.

13. Saint-Yves does indeed say that the 'Magi-Kings' came from Agarttha, but without being any more precise on this point. The names usually attributed to them are doubtless imaginary, except perhaps that of *Melki-Or*, in Hebrew 'King of the Light', which is rather significant.

14. The *Amrita* of the Hindus or the *Ambrosia* of the Greeks (two words etymologically identical), draught or food of immortality, is represented notably also by the Vedic *Soma* and the Mazdean *Haoma*.

Trees producing incorruptible gums or resins play an important role in symbolism, having in particular sometimes been taken as emblems of Christ.

Ossendowski naturally was not in a position to consider things of this order, but had he penetrated more deeply into certain matters he would at least have noticed the strict analogy obtaining between the supreme ternary of Agarttha and that of Lamaism, such as he describes it: the Dalai Lama, 'realizing the saintliness [or pure spirituality] of *Buddha*'; the *Tashi-Lama*, 'realizing his science' [not 'magic' as he appears to think but, rather, 'theurgy']; and the *Bogdo-Khan*, 'representing his material and warlike strength'—exactly the same distribution according to the 'three worlds'. He could even have drawn these parallels all the more readily since he had been informed that 'the capital of *Agharti*...reminds one of Lhasa where the palace of the Dalai Lama, the Potala, is the top [*sic*] of a mountain covered with monasteries and temples.'[15] This way of expressing things is faulty besides, for in reality it is the image that recalls its prototype, and not the converse. Now the center of Lamaism can only be an image of the true 'Center of the World'; but when the various sites of such centers are considered, it turns out that they all present certain topographical peculiarities that, far from being unimportant, have an incontestable symbolic value that must, in addition, correspond to those laws through which the 'spiritual influences' operate, which is a topic that properly belongs to the traditional science that one could call 'sacred geography'.

But there is yet another parallel that is no less remarkable. Saint-Yves, describing the different degrees or circles of the initiatic hierarchy, which are related to certain symbolic numerals referring particularly to the divisions of time, ends by saying that 'the highest circle, and the one nearest to the mysterious center, is composed of twelve parts, which represent the supreme initiation and correspond to the zodiac, among other things.' Now this composition is also found in what is known as the 'circular council' of the Dalai Lama, made up of twelve great *Namshans* (or *Nomekhans*), and moreover is also found even in certain Western traditions, notably those concerning the 'Knights of the Round Table'. We should further add that from the point of view of the cosmic order, the twelve

15. Ossendowski, *Beasts, Men and Gods*, p303.

members of the inner circle of Agarttha represent not only the twelve signs of the zodiac, but also (we are tempted to say 'rather', though the two interpretations are not mutually exclusive) the twelve *Ādityas*, which represent as many forms of the sun in relation to these same zodiacal signs,[16] and naturally, since *Manu Vaivasvata* is called 'son of the Sun', the 'King of the World' also counts the sun among his various emblems.[17]

The principal conclusion to be drawn from what has been said is that all the world over descriptions of spiritual centers that are more or less hidden (or at least accessible only with great difficulty) bear a close resemblance to each other. The only plausible explanation for this similarity is that, if the accounts refer to different centers, as seems to be true in some cases, then they must all be emanations, so to speak, from one supreme center, just as all particular traditions are finally only adaptations of the great, primordial tradition.

16. It is said that the *Ādityas* (issue of *Aditi*, or the 'Indivisible') were first seven before being twelve, and that their head was then *Varuna*. The twelve *Ādityas* are *Dhātri, Mitra, Aryaman, Rudra, Varuna, Sūrya, Bhaga, Vivasvat, Pūshan, Savitri, Tvashtri,* and *Vishnu*. They are so many manifestations of a unique and indivisible essence; and it is also said that these twelve suns will appear simultaneously at the end of the cycle, returning then into the essential and primordial unity of their common nature. Among the Greeks the twelve great gods of Olympus also correspond to the twelve signs of the zodiac.

17. The symbol to which we allude is precisely the one that Catholic liturgy attributes to Christ in applying to him the title of *Sol Justitiae*; the Word is effectively the 'spiritual Sun', that is, the true 'Center of the World'; furthermore, this expression *Sol Justitiae* refers directly to the attributes of *Melki-Tsedeq*. It should also be noted that both in antiquity and in the Middle Ages the lion, a solar animal, was an emblem of justice as well as of power; and the sign of the Lion in the zodiac is the 'house' of the sun. The sun with twelve rays may be considered to represent the twelve *Ādityas*; and from another point of view, if the sun represents Christ, the twelve rays are the twelve apostles (the word *apostolos* signifying 'sent', as the rays are also 'sent' by the sun). Moreover, in the number of the twelve apostles one can see a sign, among many others, of the perfect conformity of Christianity with the primordial tradition.

5

SYMBOLISM
OF THE GRAIL

THE KNIGHTS OF THE ROUND TABLE were mentioned in the previous chapter, and it will not be outside our purview to call attention to the significance of the 'Grail quest', which in legends of Celtic origin is presented as their principal concern. All traditions allude to something that from a certain time become lost or hidden, such as the *Soma* of the Hindus and the Persian *Haoma* or 'draught of immortality', these latter having a precise and very direct connection with the Grail, which was said to be the sacred chalice that contained the blood of Christ—another 'draught of immortality'. Elsewhere the symbolism is different, as, for example, among the Jews, where it is the pronunciation of the full divine Name that has been lost,[1] but the fundamental idea is always the same, and we will shortly see to what exactly it corresponds.

It is said that the Holy Grail is the chalice that served at the Last Supper and in which Joseph of Arimathea collected the blood and water flowing from the wound opened in Christ's side by the lance

---

1. In this regard one must also remember the 'Lost Word' of the Masons, which likewise symbolizes the secrets of true initiation; the 'search for the Lost Word' is thus but another form of the 'Grail quest', which justifies the relationship pointed out by the historian Henri Martin between the *Massenie du Saint Graal* and Masonry (see *The Esoterism of Dante*, chap. 4); and the explanations given here will facilitate an understanding of our previous discussion of the very close link between the symbolism of the Grail itself and the 'common center' of all initiatic organizations.

of the centurion Longinus.[2] According to legend, this chalice was carried to England by Joseph of Arimathea and Nicodemus,[3] indicating a link between the Celtic tradition and Christianity. The chalice in fact plays an important role in most of the ancient traditions, no doubt most notably among the Celts, and equally worth noting is its frequent association with the lance, these two symbols thus being in some way complementary; but to digress on this point would take us far from our present subject.[4]

The essential significance of the Grail is perhaps shown most clearly by what is said of its origin: it is supposed to have been fashioned by angels from an emerald that dropped from Lucifer's forehead at the time of his fall.[5] This emerald rather strikingly calls to mind the *urnā*, or frontal pearl, which in Hindu symbolism (and subsequently adopted by Buddhism) often takes the place of the third eye of *Shiva*, representing what can be called the 'sense of eternity', as we have explained elsewhere.[6] It is said too that the Grail had been entrusted to Adam in the Terrestrial Paradise, but that after his fall he lost it in turn, for he was not allowed to take it when he was driven from Eden, the significance of which should be clear, given what we have just said. Separated from his center of origin, man found himself thereafter enclosed in the temporal realm, from which he could no longer return to that unique place whence all things are contemplated under the aspect of eternity. In other

2. This name *Longinus* is related to that of the spear itself, in Greek *logké* (pronounced *lonké*); the Latin *lancea* moreover has the same root.

3. These two personages represent the royal and the sacerdotal powers respectively, and the same applies to Arthur and Merlin in the institution of the 'Round Table'.

4. We will only say that the symbolism of the lance is often related to the 'World Axis', with respect to which the blood dripping from the lance has the same significance as the dew falling from the 'Tree of Life'; besides, we know that all traditions are unanimous in affirming that the vital principle is intimately linked to the blood.

5. Some say an emerald fallen from the crown of Lucifer, but there is a confusion here deriving from the fact that before his fall Lucifer was the 'Angel of the Crown' (that is, of *Kether* [Hebrew for 'crown'], the first *Sephirah*), in Hebrew *Hakathriel*, a name moreover whose number is 666.

6. *Man and His Becoming according to the Vedānta*, chap. 20.

words, the possession of the 'sense of eternity' is linked to what all the traditions call, as we mentioned above, the 'primordial state', the restoration of which constitutes the first stage of true initiation, as it is the preliminary condition for the effective conquest of the 'supra-human' states.[7] The 'Terrestrial Paradise', moreover, properly represents the 'Center of the World', an expression that will be better understood later, when the original meaning of the word 'Paradise' is examined.

The following may appear even more enigmatic: Seth succeeded in re-entering the Terrestrial Paradise, and was thus able to recover the precious chalice; now the name 'Seth' expresses the idea of foundation or stability, and hence indicates in some way the restoration of the primordial order destroyed by man's fall.[8] One must therefore understand that both Seth and those who later possessed the Grail were thereby able to establish a spiritual center destined to replace the Lost Paradise, a kind of image of the latter, with the possession of the Grail then representing the integral preservation of the primordial tradition in such a spiritual center. The legend does not record where or by whom the Grail was preserved until the time of Christ, although the Celtic origin attributed to it suggests that the Druids had a role, and should be counted among the regular guardians of the primordial tradition.

The loss of the Grail, or of any of its symbolic equivalents, amounts to the loss of tradition, along with all that it conveys; but in fact it is more true to say that the tradition is hidden rather than lost, or at least that it can be lost only to certain secondary spiritual centers that have ceased to maintain a direct contact with the supreme center. This latter always preserves intact the deposit of the

---

7. Concerning this 'primordial' or 'edenic' state, see *The Esoterism of Dante*, chaps. 6 and 8, and *Man and His Becoming according to the Vedānta*, chap. 23.

8. It is said that Seth remained forty years in the Terrestrial Paradise, the same number also signifying 'reconciliation' or 'return to the Principle'. Periods measured by this number are often met with in the Judeo-Christian tradition: recall the forty days of the Deluge, the forty years of the Israelites' wanderings in the wilderness, the forty days Moses spent on Sinai, the forty-day fast of Christ (Lent having naturally the same significance); and more examples could doubtless be found.

tradition, and remains unaffected by any changes occurring in the outer world; thus it is that, according to various Church Fathers, notably Saint Augustine, the Deluge did not reach as far as the Terrestrial Paradise, which is the 'dwelling place of Enoch and land of saints',[9] and the summit of which 'touches the lunar sphere', that is, lies beyond the domain of change (the sublunary world), at the meeting-point of the Earth and the Heavens.[10] But, even as the Terrestrial Paradise has become inaccessible, so the supreme center, which is fundamentally the same thing, can cease to be manifested outwardly during the course of certain periods, and then it can be said that the tradition is lost to the great mass of humanity, for it is preserved only in certain strictly closed centers, so that, in contrast to the original state, the majority of people can no longer participate in it in a conscious or effective manner.[11] This is precisely the state of affairs in our present age, the beginning of which stretches back well beyond what is accessible to ordinary and 'profane' history. Thus, according to the case, the loss of tradition can be understood in this general sense, or else be related to the obscuration of the spiritual centers that more or less invisibly governed the destinies of particular peoples or civilizations; and so every instance of a symbolism that relates to it must be examined to determine in which of these two senses it should be interpreted.

From what has been said, it follows that the Grail simultaneously represents two closely related things, for anyone who possesses the 'primordial tradition' in its integrality, that is, who has attained the degree of effective knowledge that this possession essentially implies,

9. 'Enoch walked with God; and he was not [in the visible or outer world], for God took him' (Gen. 5:24). He would then have been transported to the Terrestrial Paradise; this is what certain theologians, such as Tostat and Cajetan, also believe. On the 'Land of the Saints' or the 'Land of the Living', see below.

10. This conforms with the symbolism used by Dante, who placed the Terrestrial Paradise at the summit of the mountain of Purgatory, which for him is identified with the 'polar mountain' of all traditions.

11. The Hindu tradition teaches that there was originally only one caste, called *Hamsa*, which signifies that all men at that time possessed normally and spontaneously the spiritual degree designated by this name, a degree that lies beyond the distinctions of the four present-day castes.

is thereby effectively reintegrated into the fullness of the 'primordial state'. To both these, the 'primordial state' and the 'primordial tradition', we attach the double sense inhering in the word 'Grail' itself, for by one of those verbal assimilations that play a not at all negligible role in symbolism, and that furthermore have much more profound reasons than might be imagined at first glance, the Grail is both a 'vase' (*grasale*) and a 'book' (*gradale* or *graduale*), the latter obviously signifying tradition,[12] while the first more directly concerns the state itself.

We have no intention of entering here into the secondary details of the legend of the Holy Grail, even though all of these, too, have a symbolic value, or of pursuing the history of the 'Knights of the Round Table' and their exploits; we will only point out that the 'Round Table', built by King Arthur[13] according to Merlin's specifications, was destined to receive the Grail at such time that it would be won by one of the Knights and brought back from Great Britain to Brittany. The table itself is again another of those apparently very ancient symbols that were always associated with the idea of spiritual centers as guardians of the tradition; moreover, the circular shape of the table is formally linked to the zodiac by the presence around it of twelve principal personages,[14] a detail which, as we said above, is to be found in the constitution of all such centers.

Another symbol related to an aspect of the Grail legend and deserving special attention is *Montsalvat* (literally, 'mount of salvation'), represented as rising out of the midst of the sea in an inaccessible region behind which the sun rises, its peak situated 'on distant

12. In certain versions of the legend of the Holy Grail the two meanings are closely mingled, and then the book becomes an inscription traced by Christ or an angel on the chalice itself. Associations with the 'Book of Life' and with certain elements of Apocalyptic symbolism could also easily be made here.

13. The name *Arthur* has a very remarkable meaning related to 'polar' symbolism, which we may perhaps have occasion to explain another time.

14. The 'Knights of the Round Table' sometimes number fifty (which among the Hebrews was the number of the Jubilee, and which was also related to the 'reign of the Holy Spirit'); but even then there are always twelve who play a predominant role. Recall also the twelve peers of Charlemagne in other legendary tales of the Middle Ages.

shores no mortal can approach.' It is at one and the same time the 'sacred isle' and the 'polar mountain', two equivalent symbols that will be discussed later; and it is the 'land of immortality', which is naturally identified with the Terrestrial Paradise.[15]

Returning to the Grail itself, we can easily see that its primary significance is basically the same as that of the sacred vase, wherever it is found, and which, notably in the East, is that of the sacrificial vessel that originally held the Vedic *Soma* or Mazdean *Haoma,* the 'draught of immortality' that bestows upon or restores to those who take it with the requisite disposition, the 'sense of eternity'. A separate study would be required to cover fully the symbolism of the chalice and its contents, but what has been said will lead us to other considerations of the greatest importance to the present subject.

15. The similarity between *Montsalvat* and *Meru* was pointed out to us by some Hindus, and this is what led us to examine more closely the significance of the Western legend of the Grail.

6

MELKI-TSEDEQ

EASTERN traditions relate that at a certain time the *Soma* became unknown, so that in sacrificial rites it was necessary to substitute for it another beverage that was no more than a symbol of the original;[1] this was the role played principally by wine, to which a large part of the Greek legend of *Dionysos* is devoted.[2] Now wine is often taken to represent the authentic initiatic tradition. In Hebrew the words *yayin*, 'wine', and *sod*, 'mystery', share the same number[3] and are thus interchangeable, and among the Sufis, wine symbolizes esoteric knowledge, that is, the doctrine reserved for the elite and not suitable for everyone, just as everyone cannot drink wine with impunity. It follows from this that the use of wine in a rite confers upon that rite a clearly initiatic character; such is the case notably of the 'eucharistic' sacrifice of Melchizedek, which is the essential point upon which we shall now dwell.[4]

---

1. Following the tradition of the Persians, there are two kinds of *Haoma*: the white, which could be gathered only on the 'sacred mountain', which they called *Alborj*, and the yellow, which replaced the first when the ancestors of the Iranians had left their original dwelling-place, but which subsequently was also lost. Here we have the successive phases of spiritual obscuration that occur gradually throughout the different ages of the human cycle.

2. *Dionysos*, or *Bacchus*, has many names, corresponding to as many different aspects; under at least one of these aspects, tradition has it that he came from India. The account of his having been born from the thigh of *Zeus* rests on a most curious verbal assimilation: the Greek word *meros*, 'thigh', has been substituted for the name of *Meru*, the 'polar mountain', with which it is phonetically almost identical.

3. The numerical value of each of these two words is 70.

4. Melchizedek's sacrifice is usually regarded as a 'prefiguration' of the Eucharist; and the Christian priesthood is identified with the very priesthood of Melchizedek according to the application to Christ of this verse from the Psalms:

The name Melchizedek, or more precisely *Melki-Tsedeq*, is in fact none other than the title used in the Judeo-Christian tradition to expressly designate the function of the 'King of the World'. We were somewhat hesitant to mention this fact—a fact that can help explain one of the most enigmatic passages of the Hebrew Bible— but once we decided to treat the question of the 'King of the World', we could hardly pass over it in silence. In this regard let us recall here the words of Saint Paul: 'About this we have much to say which is hard to explain, since you have become dull of hearing.'[5]

The biblical text which prompts us to make these remarks is the following: 'And Melchizedek king of Salem brought out bread and wine; he was priest of God Most High [*El Elion*]. And he blessed him and said, "Blessed be Abram[6] by God Most High, maker of heaven and earth; and blessed be God Most High, who has delivered your enemies into your hand!" And Abram gave him a tenth of everything.'[7]

Melki-Tsedeq is thus both king and priest: his name means 'King of Justice', and he is at the same time king of *Salem*, that is to say of 'Peace', so here again we find above all 'Justice' and 'Peace', which are precisely the two fundamental attributes of the 'King of the World'. It should also be pointed out that contrary to common opinion, the word *Salem* never actually designated a city, even though, taken as the symbolic name of the residence of *Melki-Tsedeq*, it can be considered the equivalent of *Agarttha*. In any case it is an error to see in it the primitive name for Jerusalem, as the latter was originally called *Jebus*; on the contrary, if the name Jerusalem was given to that city when a spiritual center was established there by the Jews, this was to indicate that from that point on it was a sort of visible image of the true Salem; and it should be noted that the Temple was built

---

Tu es sacerdos in aeternum secundum ordinem Melchissedec ['You are a priest for ever after the order of Melchizedek'] (Ps. 110:4).

5. Heb. 5:11.

6. At that time the name *Abram* had not yet been changed to *Abraham*; the name *Sarai* was changed at the same time to *Sarah* (Gen. 17), so that the sum of the numerical values remained the same.

7. Gen. 14:19–20.

by Solomon, whose name (*Shlomoh*) is also derived from *Salem*, and means 'the Peaceable One'.[8]

Let us see how Paul comments on what is said of *Melki-Tsedeq*: 'For this Melchizedek, king of Salem, priest of the Most High God, met Abraham returning from the slaughter of the kings and blessed him; and to him Abraham apportioned a tenth part of everything. He is first, by translation of his name, king of righteousness, and then he is also king of Salem, that is, king of peace. He is without father or mother or genealogy, and has neither beginning of days nor end of life, but resembling the Son of God he continues a priest for ever.'[9]

Now Melchizedek is here represented as superior to Abraham, for he blesses him, and 'it is beyond dispute that the inferior is blessed by the superior';[10] and for his part Abraham recognizes this superiority by giving the tithe, a mark of his dependence. We have here a veritable 'investiture', almost in the feudal sense of the word, but with the difference that it is a spiritual investiture; and it is here, let us add, that we find the exact point of juncture between the Hebraic tradition and the great primordial tradition. The 'blessing' spoken of is properly the communication of a 'spiritual influence' in which Abraham is henceforth to participate; and we can note that the formula that was used placed Abraham in direct relationship with the 'Most High God', whom the same Abraham afterward invokes under the name of *Jehovah*.[11] If *Melki-Tsedeq* is thus superior to Abraham, it is because the 'Most High' (*Elion*), who is the God of *Melki-Tsedek*, is himself superior to the 'All-Powerful' (*Shaddaï*), who is the God of Abraham, which is to say that the first of these two names represents a divine aspect higher than the second. Moreover, an extremely important point that seems never to have been noticed is that *El Elion* is the equivalent of *Emmanuel*, these two

8. We should note also that the same root is found again in the words *Islam* and *muslim*, 'submission to the divine Will' (which is the proper meaning of the word *Islam*) being the condition necessary for 'Peace'; the idea expressed here is comparable to that of the Hindu *Dharma*.

9. Heb. 7:1–3.

10. Ibid., 7:7.

11. Gen. 14:22.

names having exactly the same numerical value;[12] and this links the story of *Melki-Tsedeq* directly with that of the 'Magi-Kings', whose meaning we have already explained. This becomes even more evident when we recall that the priesthood of *Melki-Tsedeq* is that of *El Elion*, while the Christian priesthood is that of *Emmanuel*; if, then, *El Elion* is *Emmanuel*, these two priesthoods are in fact one, and so the Christian priesthood, which, moreover, essentially entails the eucharistic offering of bread and wine, is truly 'after the order of Melchizedek'.[13]

Judeo-Christian tradition distinguishes two priesthoods, one 'after the order of Aaron,' and the other 'after the order of Melchizedek'; the latter is superior to the former, just as Melchizedek is superior to Abraham, from whom issues the tribe of Levi, and consequently the family of Aaron.[14] This superiority is clearly affirmed by Paul, who said that 'One might even say that Levi himself, who receives tithes [from the people of Israel], paid tithes through Abraham.'[15] Although we shall not pursue this question of the significance of the two priesthoods here, these additional words of Saint Paul are worth quoting: 'Here [in the Levitical priesthood] tithes are received by mortal men; there, by one of whom it is testified that he lives.'[16] This one that 'lives', who is *Melki-Tsedeq*, is also *Manu*, of whom it can indeed be said that he 'continues a priest for ever' (in Hebrew, *le-ōlam*), that is, for the entire duration of his cycle (*Manvantara*),

12. The numerical value of each of these names is 197.

13. This is the complete justification of the identity we indicated earlier; it should be noted however that participation in the tradition may not always be conscious; in this case it is nonetheless real as a means of transmission of 'spiritual influences', though without implying effective accession to any rank whatsoever of the initiatic hierarchy.

14. On the basis of the preceding remarks it can also be said that this superiority corresponds to that of the New Covenant over the Ancient Law (Heb. 7:22). It would be opportune to explain here why Christ was born into the royal tribe of Judah and not the priestly tribe of Levi (see Heb. 7:11–17), but such considerations would lead us too far afield. The organization of the twelve tribes, descending from the twelve sons of Jacob, is naturally linked to the twelvefold constitution of the spiritual centers.

15. Heb. 7:9.

16. Ibid., 7:8.

or of the world over which he specifically rules. That is why he is without 'genealogy', for his origin is 'non-human' since he is himself the prototype of man, truly 'resembling the Son of God' since by virtue of the Law that he formulates he is for this world the very image of the divine Word.[17]

Foremost among other points that we could raise is the observation that the story of the 'Magi-Kings' presents three distinct personages, who are the three heads of the initiatic hierarchy, whereas that of *Melki-Tsedeq* presents only one, though one able to unite in himself aspects corresponding to the same three functions. This is why some have made a further distinction by identifying *Adoni-Tsedeq*, the 'Lord of Justice', as he who divides as it were into *Kohen-Tsedeq*, 'Priest of Justice', and *Melki-Tsedeq*, 'King of Justice'—these three aspects being in fact assimilable, respectively, to the functions of the *Brahātmā*, the *Mahātmā*, and the *Mahānga*.[18] Although *Melki-Tsedeq* is properly only the name of the third aspect, it is usually applied by extension to the three as a whole, and, if it is thus employed in preference to the others, this is because the function it expresses is nearest to the outer world and thus that which is manifested most immediately. It can be said moreover that the expression 'King of the World', as well as 'King of Justice', refers directly to the royal power only, and in India we also find the expression *Dharma-Rāja*, which is the literal equivalent of *Melki-Tsedeq*.[19]

---

17. In the *Pistis Sophia* of the Alexandrine Gnostics, Melchizedek is given the name 'Great Receiver of Eternal Light'; this again is in conformity with the function of *Manu*, who does in fact receive the intelligible Light by a ray emanating directly from the Principle, which he in turn reflects into the world that is his domain, this being moreover why *Manu* is called 'son of the Sun'.

18. There exist still other traditions concerning *Melki-Tsedeq*. According to one, at the age of fifty-two he was consecrated in the Terrestrial Paradise by the angel *Mikaël*. This symbolic number fifty-two moreover plays an important role in the Hindu tradition, where it is considered the total number of meanings comprised in the Veda, and it is even said that as many different pronunciations of the monosyllable *Om* correspond to these meanings.

19. This name, or rather title, of *Dharma Rāja* is applied, notably in the *Mahābhārata*, to *Yudishthira*; but it was so applied first of all to *Yama*, the 'Judge of the dead', whose very close relationship with *Manu* was previously indicated.

If we now take *Melki-Tsedek's* name in its strictest sense, the attributes proper to the 'King of Justice' are the scales and the sword, the same attributes that characterize *Mikaël*, considered as 'Angel of Judgement'.[20] In the social order these two emblems represent, respectively, the administrative and the military functions that properly belong to the Kshatriyas, and are the two elements constituting royal power. Considered hieroglyphically, they are also the two characters forming the Arabic and Hebraic root *Haq*, which signifies both 'Justice' and 'Truth',[21] and which also served to denote royalty among various ancient peoples.[22] *Haq* is the power that establishes the rule of Justice, that is, the equilibrium symbolized by the scales, whereas power itself is symbolized by the sword,[23] which is exactly what characterizes the essential role of the royal power; in the spiritual order, on the other hand, it is the power of Truth. We must add moreover that a modified form of the root *Haq* also exists, obtained by substituting the sign of spiritual power for that of material power; and since this form *Hak* properly designates 'Wisdom' (in Hebrew, *Hokmah*), it is more appropriate for sacerdotal authority, just as the other is for royal power. This is further confirmed by the fact that the two corresponding forms are found with similar meanings in the root *kan*, which in very diverse languages signifies 'power' or 'efficacy', and also 'knowledge',[24] *kan* being above all spiritual or intellectual power, identical with Wisdom (whence *Kohen*, 'priest' in Hebrew), whereas *qan* is the material power (from which are derived many words expressing the idea of 'possession', notably

20. In Christian iconography the angel *Mikaël* is figured with these two attributes in the representations of the 'Last Judgement'.

21. Likewise, among the ancient Egyptians *Mā* or *Maāt* was simultaneously 'Justice' and 'Truth'; she is seen figured on one of the pans of the Scales of Judgement, the other pan holding a vase, a hieroglyph for the heart. In Hebrew, *hoq* signifies 'decree' (Ps. 2:7).

22. The word *Haq* has the numerical value 108, which is one of the fundamental cyclical numbers. In India the Shaivite rosary is composed of 108 beads, the rosary in its primary significance symbolizing the 'chain of the worlds', that is, the causal chain of the cycles or states of existence.

23. This significance could be summarized in the formula 'might in the service of right', if modern usage had not degraded it to a wholly external meaning.

24. See *The Esoterism of Dante*, chap. 7.

the word *Qaïn*.[25] These roots and their derivatives could no doubt give rise to many other considerations, but we shall have to restrict ourselves here to what bears most directly on the subject at hand.

We may complete this line of thought by recalling that the Hebrew Kabbalah states that the *Shekinah* is represented in the 'inferior world' by the last of the ten Sephiroth, called *Malkuth*, meaning 'Kingdom', a designation of particular interest from our present point of view; but even more interesting is the fact that among the synonyms sometimes given for *Malkuth*, we find *Tsedeq*, or 'the Just'.[26] This convergence of *Malkuth* and *Tsedeq*, or of Royalty (the government of the world) and Justice, is met with again precisely in the name *Melki-Tsedeq*. In this context it represents the distributive and rightly balanced Justice found in the 'middle column' of the sephirothic tree; it must be distinguished from the Justice opposed to Mercy, which is identified with Rigor in the 'left-hand column', for these are two different aspects (which Hebrew distinguishes, respectively, by the words *Tsedaqah* and *Din*). It is the first of these that denotes 'Justice' in both the strictest and the most complete sense of the word, implying essentially the idea of balance or harmony and indissolubly linked with 'Peace'.

Malkuth is the 'reservoir where the waters that flow from the river on high, that is to say all the emanations (graces or spiritual influences) that are poured out so abundantly,'[27] reunite. This 'river on high' and the waters that descend from it are strangely reminiscent of the role attributed to the celestial river *Gangā* in the Hindu tradition; and one could also say that *Shakti*, of which the *Gangā* is an

25. The word *Khan*, a title given to leaders by the peoples of Central Asia, is perhaps related to the same root.

26. *Tsedeq* is also the name of the planet Jupiter, whose angel is called *Tsadqiel-Melek*; the similarity with the name *Melki-Tsedeq* (to which has been added only *El*, the divine name that forms the ending common to all angelic names) is here too evident to require emphasis. In India, the same planet is called *Brihaspati*, which is equally the 'Celestial Pontiff'.

Another synonym for *Malkuth* is *Sabbath*, whose sense of 'rest' obviously refers to the idea of 'Peace', all the more as this idea expresses, as we have seen above, the external aspect of the *Shekinah* herself, that aspect by which she communicates herself to the 'inferior world'.

27. P. Vulliaud, *La Kabbale juive*, I, p509.

aspect, is not without analogy to the *Shekinah*, were it only by reason of the 'providential' function common to them both. The reservoir of the celestial waters is naturally identical with the spiritual center of our world, from which the four rivers of *Pardes* make their way toward the four cardinal points. The Jews identify the spiritual center with Mount Zion, calling it the 'Heart of the World', a designation that is in any case common to all 'Holy Lands' and that for them becomes somewhat equivalent to the *Meru* of the Hindus or the *Alborj* of the Persians.[28] 'The Tabernacle of the Holiness of *Jehovah*, the residence of the *Shekinah*, is the Holy of Holies, that is, the heart of the Temple, which is itself the center of Zion (Jerusalem) just as Holy Zion is the center of the Land of Israel, and as the Land of Israel is the center of the world.'[29] This can be pushed even further, not only by listing every name enumerated above in an inverse order, but also by adding after the Tabernacle in the Temple, the Ark of the Covenant in the Tabernacle, and then, on the Ark of the Covenant itself, the place where the *Shekinah* is manifested (between the two *Cherubim*)—all this representing so many successive approximations to the 'spiritual Pole'.

Dante depicts Jerusalem as the 'spiritual Pole' in precisely this way, as we have explained elsewhere,[30] but the moment we leave behind the strictly Judaic point of view, this Pole becomes primarily symbolic and does not constitute a localization in the strict sense of the word. All the secondary spiritual centers, constituted with a view to adaptions of the primordial tradition to determined conditions, are, as we have already shown, images of the supreme center; in reality Zion can only be one of these secondary centers, although it may still be identified symbolically with the supreme center by reason of this similarity. Jerusalem, as its name indicates, is indeed

---

28. Among the Samaritans, it is the mountain *Gerizim* that plays the same role and receives the same names; it is the 'Blessed Mountain', the 'Eternal Hill', the 'Mount of the Heritage', the 'House of God' and the Tabernacle of his Angels, the dwelling-place of the *Shekinah*; it is even identified with the 'Primordial Mountain' (*Har Qadim*), where *Eden* was, and which was not submerged by the waters of the Deluge.

29. P. Vulliaud, *La Kabbale juive*, I, p509.

30. *The Esoterism of Dante*, chap. 8.

an image of the true *Salem*; and what has been said and will be said further about the 'Holy Land' (which is not merely the Land of Israel) will help us to understand this point without difficulty.

In this connection, another very remarkable expression used as a synonym for the 'Holy Land' is the 'Land of the Living': it obviously designates the 'abode of immortality' and so is applicable, strictly speaking, to the Terrestrial Paradise or its symbolic equivalents; but this name was also carried over to the secondary 'Holy Lands', notably the Land of Israel. It is said that the 'Land of the Living comprises seven lands', about which Vulliaud observes that 'this land is Canaan, in which there were seven peoples.'[31] No doubt this is correct in the literal sense, but symbolically these seven lands —as also those in the Islamic tradition—could equally well correspond to the seven *dvīpas* which, according to Hindu tradition, have *Meru* as a common center, a point to which we shall return. There is also a striking resemblance, which can hardly be accidental, between the epochs of the seven *Manus* (counting from the beginning of this *kalpa* up to the present age)[32] and the former worlds, or the creations prior to our own, represented by the 'seven kings of Edom', the number seven in this context referring to the seven 'days' of Genesis.

---

31. *La Kabbale juive*, II, p 116.

32. A *Kalpa* comprises fourteen *Manvantaras*; *Vaivasvata*, the present *Manu*, is the seventh of this *Kalpa*, called *Shrī-Shveta-Varāha-Kalpa*, or 'Era of the White Boar'. Another curious thing to note is that the Jews call Rome *Edom*; now, tradition also speaks of seven kings of Rome, the second of these being *Numa*, who is considered the legislator of the city and bears a name that is not only the exact syllabic reversal of *Manu*, but that can also be related to the Greek *nomos*, 'law'. There are thus grounds for believing that from a certain point of view the seven kings of Rome are only a particular representation of the seven *Manus* for a given civilization, just as the seven sages of Greece, when similarly viewed, are a representation of the seven *Rishis*, in whom is synthesized the wisdom of the cycle immediately preceding our own.

7

LUZ:
ABODE OF
IMMORTALITY

Traditions telling of a 'subterranean world' are found among many peoples, and we do not intend to collect them all here, especially since some do not seem to have any direct relevance to our topic. It is worth noting in a general way, however, that the 'cult of the caverns' is always more or less linked to the idea of an 'interior place', or a 'central place', and that in this connection the symbol of the cave and that of the heart closely converge.[1] On the other hand, in Central Asia, as in America and possibly elsewhere, there actually are caverns and underground sites where certain initiatic centers have been able to persist for centuries. But aside from these particular facts, from all that has been reported on this subject it is not difficult to distill a certain symbolism; indeed, we can even say that it is precisely considerations of a symbolic nature that have determined the choice of these subterranean locations for the establishment of initiatic centers, much more than any simple reasons of prudence. Perhaps Saint-Yves may have been able to explain this symbolism, but he failed to do so, and this is what lends the appearance of fantasy to certain portions of his work.[2] As for

1. The cave, or the grotto, represents the cavity of the heart considered as the center of the being, and also the interior of the 'World Egg'.
2. For example the passage that tells of the 'descent to the hells'; this may be compared with what was said on the same subject in *The Esoterism of Dante*.

Ossendowski, he was surely not capable of going beyond what he had been told, and of seeing in it any but the most literal meaning.

Among the traditions alluded to above is one of particular interest, which is found in Judaism, and concerns a mysterious city called *Luz*.[3] This name was originally that of the place where Jacob had his dream, and which he subsequently called *Beith-El*, or 'House of God',[4] a point to which we shall return. It is said that the 'Angel of Death' could not enter this city, and wielded no power over it; and, by a rather singular and very significant convergence, some locate it near *Alborj*, which is likewise the 'abode of immortality' for the Persians.

Near *Luz* there is purported to be an almond tree (also called *luz* in Hebrew), at the base of which is a hollow through which one enters an underground passage;[5] this passage leads to the city itself, which remains completely hidden. Moreover, in its various meanings the word *luz* appears to be derived from a root denoting everything that is hidden, covered, enveloped, silent, and secret; and it is interesting to note that words designating the heavens originally had the same meaning. We usually equate *coelum* [Latin for 'heaven/sky'] with the Greek *koilon*, or 'hollow' (which may also have some connection with the cavern, especially since Varro indicates this relationship with the expression *a cavo coelum*); but we must also note that the oldest and most accurate form is judged to be *caelum*, which recalls very closely the verb *caelare*, 'to hide'. In Sanskrit, moreover, *Varuna* derives from the root *var*, 'to cover' (which is also the meaning of the root *kal*, related in turn to the Latin *celare*, another form of *caelare*, and to its Greek synonym *kaluptein*);[6] and

3. The information given here has been partially drawn from the *Jewish Encyclopaedia* (viii, 219).

4. Gen. 28:19.

5. The traditions of certain peoples of North America also tell of a tree by means of which some men who originally lived in the interior of the earth succeeded in reaching its surface, whereas other men of the same race are said to have remained in the subterranean world. It is likely that Bulwer-Lytton was inspired by these traditions in his *Vril: The Power of the Coming Race*.

6. Other Latin words derive from the same root *kal*, such as *caligo* and perhaps the compound *occultus*. From another point of view, it is possible that the form

the Greek *Ouranos* is only another form of the same noun, *var* easily changing to *ur*. These words thus signify 'that which covers',[7] 'that which conceals',[8] or 'that which is hidden', and this last has a double sense: considered as what is hidden from the senses, it is the supra-sensible realm, but during periods of darkness or obscuration it is the tradition, now no longer externally and openly manifested—the 'celestial world' thus becoming the 'subterranean world'.

There is yet another connection to be made with the heavens: *Luz* is called the 'blue city', and the color blue, which is that of the sapphire,[9] is the celestial color. In India it is said that the blue color of the atmosphere is produced by the reflection of light on the southern face of *Meru*, which looks out upon the *Jambu-dvīpa* and is made of sapphire. This obviously refers to the same symbolism. Moreover, the *Jambu-dvīpa* represents not only India in the usual sense, but in reality also the entire terrestrial world in its present state, and in fact this world can be regarded as situated entirely to the south of *Meru*, since the latter is identified with the North Pole.[10] The seven *dvīpas* (literally, 'islands' or 'continents') emerge

---

caelare came originally from a different root *caed*, meaning 'to cut' or 'to divide' (from which also *cadere*), and consequently 'to separate' and 'to hide'; but in any case the ideas expressed by these roots are, as can be seen, very close to each other, and this could easily have given rise to the assimilation of *caelare* and *celare*, even if these two forms are etymologically independent.

7. The 'Roof of the World', which can be assimilated to the 'Celestial Land' or 'Land of the Living', has in the traditions of Central Asia a close connection with the 'Western Sky' where *Avalokiteshvara* reigns. In regard to the sense of 'covering', the Masonic expression 'under cover' should be recalled, the star-bedecked ceiling of the Lodge representing the celestial vault.

8. This is the veil of *Isis*, or of *Neith* among the Egyptians, and the 'blue veil' of the universal Mother in the Far-Eastern tradition (*Tao Te Ching*, chap. 6); applying this meaning to the visible sky will give an intimation of the role of astronomical symbolism in hiding or 'revealing' higher truths.

9. The sapphire plays an important role in biblical symbolism, appearing with particular frequency in the visions of prophets.

10. In Sanskrit the North is called *Uttara*, that is, the highest region, the South being called *Dakshina*, the region to the right, that is, on one's right hand when facing the East. *Uttarāyana* is the upward march of the sun toward the North, beginning with the winter solstice and ending at the summer solstice; *dakshināyana* is

successively during the course of certain cyclical periods, so that each is the terrestrial world envisaged in the corresponding period; they form a lotus having *Meru* as the center, with respect to which they are oriented according to the seven regions of space.[11] One face of *Meru* is thus turned toward each of the seven *dvīpas*, and if each of these faces is one of the colors of the rainbow,[12] the synthesis of these will be the color white, which is universally attributed to the supreme spiritual authority,[13] and which is the color of *Meru* considered in itself (we shall see that it is indeed called the 'white

the downward march of the sun toward the South, beginning with the summer solstice and ending at the winter solstice.

11. In Hindu symbolism (which Buddhism has retained in its legend of the 'seven steps'), the seven regions of space consist of the four cardinal points, the Zenith, and the Nadir, and finally the center itself; and note that their representation forms a cross in three dimensions (six directions, opposed two by two starting from the center). Similarly, in kabbalistic symbolism the 'Holy Palace' or 'Interior Palace' is at the center of the six directions, and thus forms the septenary, and 'Clement of Alexandria says that from God, "heart of the universe", proceed the indefinite expanses directed, one upward, one downward, this one to the right, that one to the left, one forward, and the other one backward; directing His gaze toward these six expanses as toward a number that is ever the same, He completes the world; He is the Beginning and the End [the *alpha* and the *omega*]; in Him are accomplished the six phases of time, and it is from Him that they receive their indefinite extension—that is the secret of the number seven' (quoted by Vulliaud, *La Kabbale juive*, I, pp215–16). All this is related to the development of the primordial point in space and in time. The six phases of time, corresponding respectively to the six directions of space, are six cyclical periods, subdivisions of another, more general period, and sometimes represented symbolically as six millennia; they are also assimilable to the first six 'days' of Genesis, the seventh, or *Sabbath*, representing the phase of the return to the Principle, that is, to the center. We thus have seven periods, to which can perhaps be related the respective manifestations of the seven *dvīpas*; if each of these periods is a *Manvantara*, the *Kalpa* comprises two complete septenary periods; and the same symbolism is clearly applicable to different degrees, according to the greater or lesser duration of the cyclical period envisaged.

12. See our earlier remarks on the symbolism of the rainbow. There are in reality only six colors, ranged in complementary pairs, and corresponding to the six directions in the same way, the seventh color being nothing other than white itself, just as the seventh region is identified with the center.

13. It is therefore not without reason that in the Catholic hierarchy the pope is attired in white.

mountain'), whereas the other colors only represent its aspects in relation to the different *dvīpas*. It may seem that *Meru* occupies a different position during the period of manifestation of each *dvīpa*, but in reality it is immovable because it is the center, and it is the orientation of the terrestrial world with respect to it that changes from one period to the next.

Let us return to the Hebrew word *luz*, the many different meanings of which merit careful attention. In the ordinary sense it means 'almond' (as well as 'almond tree', designating by extension both the tree and its fruit) or 'kernel'; now, the kernel is what is innermost or most hidden, and it is completely enclosed, from which stems the idea of 'inviolability'[14] (which is also found in the name Agarttha). But *luz* is also the name given to an indestructible corporeal particle, symbolically represented as an extremely hard bone, to which the soul, after death, remains linked until the resurrection.[15] As the kernel contains the germ and as the bone contains the marrow, so this *luz* contains the virtual elements necessary for the restoration of the being; and this restoration will be effected under the influence of a 'celestial dew' that will revivify the dry bones. Saint Paul alludes to this in the clearest possible way when he says: 'It is sown in dishonor, it is raised in glory.'[16] Here, as elsewhere, 'glory' refers to the *Shekinah*, here envisaged in the superior world, and to which the 'celestial dew' is closely related, as was noted earlier. *Luz*, being imperishable,[17] is the 'kernel of immortality' in the human being, just as the city that is designated by the same name is the 'abode of immortality': this is where the power of the 'Angel of Death' stops in

14. This is why the almond tree was taken as the symbol of the Virgin.

15. It is curious to note that this Jewish tradition very probably inspired certain theories of Leibnitz concerning the 'animal' (that is, the living being) subsisting perpetually with a body, though reduced to a 'miniature' after death.

16. 1 Cor. 15:42. In these words there is a strict application of the law of analogy, 'As above, so below, but inversely.'

17. In Sanskrit, the word *akshara* signifies 'indissoluble', hence 'imperishable' or 'indestructible'; it designates the syllable, the primary element and germ of language, and applies pre-eminently to the monosyllable *Om*, which is said to contain within itself the essence of the triple Veda.

both cases. It is a sort of egg or embryo of the immortal;[18] it may also be compared with the chrysalis from which the butterfly emerges,[19] a comparison which exactly conveys its role with respect to the resurrection.

The *luz* is said to be located toward the lower end of the spinal column; this might seem rather strange, but becomes clear when it is compared with what the Hindu tradition says about the power called *Kundalinī*,[20] which is a form of *Shakti* considered as immanent in the human being.[21] This force is represented by the figure of a coiled snake in a region of the subtle body corresponding precisely to the base of the spinal column; this at least is the case in the ordinary man, but by means of practices such as those of *Hatha-Yoga*, it is aroused, uncoils, and ascends through the 'wheels' (*chakras*) or 'lotuses' (*kamalas*) that correspond to the various plexuses, to reach finally the region corresponding to the 'third eye', that is, the frontal eye of *Shiva*. This stage represents the restoration of the 'primordial state', in which man recovers the 'sense of eternity', thereby attaining what we have elsewhere called 'virtual immortality'. Up to this point we are still in the human state; in a subsequent phase the *Kundalinī* finally reaches the crown of the head,[22] and this last phase relates to the effective conquest of the higher states of the being. What seems to follow from this comparison is that the location of

18. We find its equivalent in other forms in diverse traditions, and particularly, with some very important developments, in Taoism. In this regard, it is the analogue, in the 'microcosmic' order, to the 'World Egg' in the 'macrocosmic' order, since it contains the possibilities of the 'future cycle' (the *vita venturi saeculi* ['life of the world to come'] of the Catholic Creed).

19. Reference can be made to the Greek symbolism of *Psyche*, which rests for the most part on this similarity (see *Psyché*, by F. Pron).

20. The word *kundalī* (*kundalinī* in the feminine) means 'coiled in the form of a ring or spiral', this coiled condition symbolizing the embryonic or 'undeveloped' state.

21. In this respect, and from a certain point of view, its abode is also identified with the cavity of the heart; we have already referred to the relationship existing between the Hindu *Shakti* and the Hebrew *Shekinah*.

22. This is the *Brahma-randhra*, or the orifice of *Brahma*, point of contact of the *sushumnā* or 'coronal artery' with the 'solar ray'; this symbolism is discussed in detail in *Man and His Becoming according to the Vedānta*.

the *luz* in the lower part of the organism refers only to the condition of 'fallen man'; and for terrestrial humanity considered as a whole the same could be said of the location of the supreme spiritual center in the 'subterranean world'.[23]

23. All this is closely related with the real significance of the well-known Hermetic saying *Visita inferiora terrae, rectificando invenies occultum, lapidem, veram medicinam* [Visit the inferior regions of the earth; in rectitude will you find the hidden thing, the stone, the true medicine], which gives, by acrostic, the word *Vitriolum*. The 'philosophers' stone' is at the same time, and under another aspect, the 'true medicine', that is, the 'elixir of long life', which is nothing other than the 'draught of immortality'. *Interiora* is sometimes written in place of *inferiora*, but this does not alter the general meaning, as there remains the same manifest allusion to the 'subterranean world'.

8

THE SUPREME CENTER
CONCEALED DURING
THE *KALI-YUGA*

AGARTTHA, it is said, was not in fact always underground, and will not always remain so. According to Ossendowski's report, a time will come when 'the peoples of Agharti will come up from their subterranean caverns to the surface of the earth.'[1] Before its disappearance from the visible world, this center bore another name, for 'Agarttha', which means 'imperceptible' or 'inaccessible' (and also 'inviolable', since it is Salem, the 'Abode of Peace'), would not yet have been appropriate; Ossendowski clearly states that it withdrew underground 'more than six thousand years ago,' indicating thereby a date which, as it happens, very closely approximates the beginning of the *Kali-Yuga* or 'dark age' (the 'iron age' of the ancient West), which is the last of the four periods into which the *Manvantara* is divided;[2] its reappearance is to coincide with the ending of this same period.

---

1. Ossendowski, *Beasts, Men and Gods*, p314. These are the concluding words of a prophecy that the 'King of the World' is said to have made in 1890, when he appeared at the monastery of Narabanchi.

2. The *Manvantara*, or era of a *Manu*, also called *Mahā-Yuga*, comprises four *Yugas* or secondary periods: the *Krita-Yuga* (or *Satya-Yuga*), the *Tretā-Yuga*, the *Dvāpara-Yuga*, and the *Kali-Yuga*, which are identified respectively with the 'age of gold', the 'age of silver', the 'age of bronze', and the 'age of iron' of Greco-Roman antiquity. In the succession of these periods there is a kind of progressive materialization resulting from the gradual distancing from the Principle that necessarily accompanies the development of the cyclical manifestation in the corporeal world, starting from the 'primordial state'.

We have already mentioned the allusions in all traditions to something that is lost or hidden,[3] which is represented under various symbols; taken in the general sense that concerns terrestrial humanity as a whole, this loss corresponds precisely to the conditions of humanity during the *Kali-Yuga*. The present period is therefore one of obscuration and confusion;[4] its conditions are such that, as long as they endure, initiatic knowledge must necessarily remain hidden, and this explains the character of the Mysteries of 'historical' antiquity (which in fact does not even reach back to the beginning of this period)[5] and the secret societies of all peoples. Such organizations transmit an effective initiation wherever a true traditional doctrine still subsists, but offer no more than its pale shadow when the spirit of this doctrine has ceased to vivify the symbols that are only its outward representation; this happens when for various reasons all conscious connection with the spiritual center of the world has finally been broken. This is the more particular meaning of the loss of tradition as concerns specific secondary centers, which consists in a rupture of effective relations with the supreme center.

Thus, as we have already said, one should speak of something that is hidden rather than of something truly lost, for it is not lost to everyone, and some few still possess it in its integrality; and if such is the case, others always have the possibility of recovering it provided they search for it in the right way, which is to say that their intention must be directed so that through the harmonic vibrations

3. See especially chap. 5. ED.

4. In biblical symbolism the beginning of this age is notably represented by the Tower of Babel and the 'confusion of tongues'. One could quite logically think that the Fall and the Deluge correspond to the end of the first two ages, but in reality the starting-point of the Hebrew tradition does not coincide with the beginning of the *Manvantara*. It must not be forgotten that the cyclical laws are applicable in different degrees and for periods of unequal extent, periods that also sometimes encroach upon each other; hence the complications that may at first sight seem inextricable and that can be resolved only by considering the order of hierarchic subordination of the corresponding traditional centers.

5. It appears that proper notice has never been taken of the fact that historians generally find it impossible to establish an accurate chronology for anything prior to the sixth century before the Christian era.

it awakens, according to the law of 'concordant actions and reactions',[6] they are enabled to establish an effective spiritual communication with this supreme center.[7] In all traditional forms, this directing of the intention is, moreover, always symbolically represented by ritual orientation; properly speaking, the latter is in fact the direction toward some spiritual center, which, no matter what particular center it may be, is always an image of the true 'Center of the World'.[8] But the further the *Kali-Yuga* progresses, the more difficult it becomes to establish contact with this center, which becomes increasingly more closed and hidden at the same time that these secondary centers representing it externally become increasingly more rare;[9] yet when this period comes to an end the tradition will be manifested anew in its integrality, for the beginning of each *Manvantara*, coinciding with the end of the preceding one, necessarily implies for terrestrial humanity the return to the 'primordial state'.[10]

In Europe, every consciously established link with the center by means of regular organizations is now broken, and this has been so for several centuries; moreover, this rupture was not accomplished

6. This expression has been borrowed from Taoist doctrine; also, we take the word 'intention' here in a sense exactly equivalent to that of the Arabic *niyah*, which is usually translated thus, conforming in this with the Latin etymology (from *intendere*, 'to tend toward').

7. What we have just said allows us to interpret with great precision the Gospel saying 'And I tell you, ask, and it will be given you; knock, and it will be opened to you' (Luke 11:9). Here one must naturally refer to the earlier discussion concerning 'right intention' and 'good will', which will at the same time make clear the meaning of the expression *Pax in terra hominibus bonae voluntatis* ['Peace on earth to men of good will'].

8. In Islam, this orientation (*qiblah*) is something like the materialization, if we may put it so, of intention (*niyah*). The orientation of Christian churches is another particular case essentially related to the same idea.

9. Here only a relative exteriorization is meant, of course, for these secondary centers have themselves been more or less strictly closed since the beginning of the *Kali-Yuga*.

10. This is the manifestation of the Celestial Jerusalem, which, with respect to the cycle that is ending, is the same thing that the Terrestrial Paradise is with respect to the cycle that is beginning, as we explained in *The Esoterism of Dante*.

all at once, but in many successive stages.[11] The first stage dates from the beginning of the fourteenth century; what we have already said elsewhere makes it understandable that one of the principal roles of the Orders of Chivalry was to assure communication between East and West, the true importance of which will be readily grasped when it is recalled that the center here in question has always been depicted as located somewhere in the East, at least with respect to 'historical' times. Nevertheless, after the destruction of the Order of the Templars, the Brotherhood of the Rose-Cross (or what was later to be given that name) continued to assure this same communication, albeit in a more hidden way.[12] The Renaissance and the Reformation marked a new critical phase, after which, as Saint-Yves appears to suggest, came the complete and final rupture, coinciding with the Treaties of Westphalia that, in 1648, ended the Thirty Years War. Now it is remarkable that numerous writers have affirmed precisely that the true Brotherhood of the Rose-Cross left Europe shortly after the Thirty Years War to withdraw into Asia; and in this regard we recall that the Rosicrucian adepts were twelve in number, as were the members of the innermost circle of Agarttha, in conformity with the constitution common to so many other spiritual centers formed in the image of that supreme center.

Since this last period, the deposit of effective initiatic knowledge has not truly been preserved by any Western organization; thus, Swedenborg declared that the 'Lost Word' must henceforth be sought among the sages of Tibet and of Tartary; and according to the visions of Anne-Catherine Emmerich, the mysterious place that she calls the 'Mountain of Prophets'[13] is also set in the same regions. And let us add that the fragmentary information Madame Blavatsky

---

11. In the same way, from another and broader point of view, there are for human beings degrees in their remoteness from the primordial center, and it is to these degrees that the distinction of the different *Yugas* corresponds.

12. Here again we must refer to our study *The Esoterism of Dante*, where we have given everything necessary to justify this assertion.

13. Anne Catherine Emmerich (1774–1824), who was born in Westphalia and became an Augustinian nun in 1803, apparently lived from early childhood with almost continual inner visions of scenes from the Old and New Testaments. Upon the disbanding of the convents in 1811, the chroncially ill Anne Catherine withdrew

was able to gather on this subject, though without fully understanding its true significance, gave rise to her idea of the 'Great White
Lodge', which we would call, not an image, but quite simply a cari-
cature or fanciful parody of Agarttha.[14]

to a small room in Dülmen, where in 1812 she received the *stigmata*. In 1818 the
well-known poet of the German Romantic movement, Clemens Brentano, paid her
a visit, whereupon she immediately recognized him as the 'pilgrim' sent to record
her visions, a task he soon undertook. The recorded visions were eventually orga-
nized and published in several collections, those in English being (in various editions): the four-volume *The Life of Christ and Biblical Revelations of Anne Catherine
Emmerich*, and two separate compilations, one focusing on the Virgin Mary, entitled *The Life of the Blessed Virgin Mary*, and the other treating in great detail the
events surrounding the Passion, entitled *The Dolorous Passion of Our Lord Jesus
Christ*. Anne Catherine's visions are remarkable in their apparent factual accuracy,
which has even been confirmed by archeologists, the best-known case being that of
the discovery of the 'House of the Virgin' in Ephesus. The passage Guénon cites
here regarding the 'Mountain of the Prophets', is found in the Very Reverend Carl
E. Schmöger's *The Life of Anne Catherine Emmerich*, vol. 1 (Rockford, IL: Tan Books
and Publishers, 1976), chap. XLI. Of particular interest in the present context is
Anne Catherine's observation in that chapter, regarding the top of this 'Mountain
of the Prophets', that 'the whole country was like a beautiful green island up in the
clouds.' ED.

14. Those who have followed the considerations set forth here will understand
why we cannot possibly take seriously the many pseudo-initiatic organizations that
have sprung up in the contemporary West, not one of which, if put to the test—and
not even a very strict test at that—could furnish the least proof of 'regularity'.

9

THE *OMPHALOS*
AND SACRED STONES

ACCORDING TO OSSENDOWSKI'S REPORT, the 'King of the World'
formerly appeared several times in India and in Siam, 'and blessed
the people with a golden apple with the figure of a Lamb above it';[1]
and this detail takes on great importance when compared with what
Saint-Yves says of the 'cycle of the Lamb and the Ram'.[2] From
another point of view, it is even more remarkable that in Christian
symbolism there exist innumerable representations of the Lamb on
a mountain from which flow four rivers that are clearly identical
with the four rivers of the Terrestrial Paradise.[3] Now we have said
that Agarttha bore a different name prior to the onset of the *Kali-
Yuga*, and that this name was *Paradesha*, which in Sanskrit means
'supreme country', and which applies well to the spiritual center par
excellence, also called the 'Heart of the World'; it is from this word
that the Chaldeans formed *Pardes*, and the Westerners *Paradise*.

---

1. Ossendowski, *Beasts, Men and Gods*, p310.

2. It is worth reminding the reader of references made elsewhere to the connection between the Vedic *Agni* and the symbolism of the Lamb (*The Esoterism of
Dante*, chap. 8, and *Man and His Becoming according to the Vedānta*, chap. 3), in
India the ram representing the vehicle of *Agni*. Furthermore, as Ossendowski
repeatedly points out, the cult of *Rāma* still exists in Mongolia, so that there is
something other than Buddhism there, contrary to what most of the orientalists
claim. From another source we have heard of memories of the 'Cycle of Ram' that
still linger in Cambodia to this day, a piece of information so extraordinary that we
have preferred not to rely upon it, and that we mention only for the record.

3. Note also the representations of the Lamb on the book of seven seals mentioned in the Apocalypse; Tibetan lamaism also possesses seven mysterious seals, a
coincidence that we do not think can be purely accidental.

Such is the original meaning of this latter, which should make clear why we said before that in one form or another it always signifies the same thing as the *Pardes* of the Hebrew Kabbalah.

Moreover, referring back to what was said earlier concerning the symbolism of the 'Pole', it is also easy to see that the mountain of the Terrestrial Paradise is identical with the 'polar mountain', which, under various names, exists in almost all traditions. We have already mentioned the *Meru* of the Hindus and the *Alborj* of the Persians, as well as *Montsalvat* of the Western legend of the Grail; there are also the mountain *Qāf* [4] of the Arabs and the Greek *Olympus*, which in many ways have the same significance. The region in question is always one that, like the Terrestrial Paradise, has become inaccessible to ordinary humanity, and lies beyond the reach of all cataclysms that wrack the human world at the end of certain cyclical periods. This region is the veritable 'supreme country'; moreover, according to certain Vedic and Avestan texts, its location must originally have been polar, even in the literal sense of the word; and whatever its location may have been during the different phases of human history, it always remains polar in the symbolic sense, for it essentially represents the fixed axis around which the revolution of all things is accomplished.

The mountain naturally represents the 'Center of the World' before the onset of the *Kali-Yuga*, that is to say when it existed openly as it were, and was not yet subterranean; it thus corresponded to what might be called its normal position, apart from the period of obscuration the particular conditions of which imply a sort of reversal of the established order. It must also be added that apart from these considerations referring to cyclical laws, the symbols of the mountain and the cave each have their own raison d'être, and are truly complementary; [5] moreover, the cave may be envisaged

---

4. It is said that the mountain *Qāf* cannot be reached 'either by land or by sea' (*lā bil-barr wa lā bil-baḥr*; compare what was said earlier of *Montsalvat*), and among its other names is 'Mountain of the Saints' (*Jabal al-Awliyā*), which can be related to the 'Mountain of the Prophets' of Anne-Catherine Emmerich.

5. This complementarism is that of two triangles placed inversely one upon the other, in this way forming the 'seal of Solomon'; it is also comparable to that of the spear and of the cup mentioned earlier, and to many other equivalent symbols.

as located in the interior of the mountain itself, or as immediately beneath it.

There are still other symbols in ancient traditions that represent the 'Center of the World', one of the most remarkable perhaps being the *Omphalos*,[6] which is likewise found among nearly all peoples. In Greek the word means 'umbilicus' or 'navel', but it also designates in a general way all that is central, and in particular the hub of a wheel; in Sanskrit the word *nābhi* has the same connotations, as do various words in the Celtic and Germanic languages derived from the same root, which is then found under the forms *nab* and *nav*.[7] In Welsh, on the other hand, the word *nav* or *naf*, which is obviously related to the forms just mentioned, carries the sense of 'chief' and is sometimes even applied to God; and so it is indeed the idea of the central Principle that is being expressed here.[8] The meaning 'hub' has, besides, a very particular importance in this regard, because the wheel is everywhere a symbol of the world accomplishing its rotation around a fixed point, a symbol that must thus be compared to the *swastika*; but in the latter the circumference representing manifestation is not depicted, so that it is the center itself that is expressly pointed to, the *swastika* then being not a representation of the world but rather of the action of the Principle in relation to the world.

6. In a work entitled *Omphalos, eine Philologische, Archäologische, Volkskundliche Abhandlung über die Vorstellungen der Griechen und Anderer Völker vom 'Nabel der Erde'* (Leipzig: B.G. Teubner, 1913), W.H. Roscher has assembled a considerable number of documents establishing this fact for the most diverse peoples; but he is in error when he claims that this symbol is linked to the conceptions of peoples concerning the shape of the earth, for he imagined it to be a question of a belief in a center on the surface of the earth in the most grossly literal sense, an opinion that implies a complete misunderstanding of the profound meaning of the symbolism. In what follows we shall make use of certain particulars found in a study by J. Loth entitled 'L'Omphalos chez les Celtes', published in *La Revue des Études anciennes* (July–September 1915).

7. In German *Nabe*, 'hub', and *Nabel*, 'navel'; similarly, in English, *nave* and *navel*, this last word having also the general meaning of center or middle. The Greek *omphalos* and the Latin *umbilicus* derive moreover from a simple modification of the same root.

8. In the Rig-Veda *Agni* is called the 'Navel of the Universe', which comes back to the same idea; the *swastika* is often, as we have already said, a symbol of *Agni*.

The symbol of the *Omphalos* could be situated in a place that was simply the center of a determined region, the spiritual center of course, rather than the geographical one, although in certain cases the two might coincide; in cases where the latter held true, this was because, for the people who inhabited the region in question, the place concerned was truly the visible image of the 'Center of the World', just as the tradition proper to that people was only an adaptation of the primordial tradition, expressed in a form that best fitted its mentality and its conditions of existence. The *Omphalos* that is best known is the one in the temple at Delphi, which was quite certainly the spiritual center of all ancient Greece;[9] and without dwelling on all the reasons that could justify the assertion, we will only note that it was at Delphi that the twice yearly Council of the Amphictyons assembled. This Council was composed of representatives from all the Hellenic peoples, and moreover formed the only effective link between these peoples, the strength of which link lay in its essentially traditional character.

The physical representation of the *Omphalos* was generally a sacred stone, commonly called a 'baetyl', a word that seems to be none other than the Hebrew *Beith-El*, or 'House of God', the name given by Jacob to the place where the Lord appeared to him in a dream: 'Then Jacob awoke from his sleep and said, "Surely the Lord is in this place; and I did not know it." And he was afraid, and said, "How awesome is this place! This is none other than the House of God, and this is the gate of heaven." So Jacob rose early in the morning and he took the stone which he had put under his head and set it up for a pillar and poured oil on the top of it. He called the name of that place Bethel [*Beith-El*], but the name of the city was Luz at first.'[10] We have explained the meaning of the word *Luz* above; moreover, it is also said that *Beith-El*, 'House of God', later became *Beith-Lehem*, 'house of bread', which is the city where Christ was

9. There were other spiritual centers in Greece, but they were more particularly reserved for initiation into the Mysteries, such centers as Eleusis and Samothrace, whereas Delphi had a social role concerned directly with the entirety of the Hellenic collectivity.

10. Gen. 28:16–19.

born;[11] and the symbolic relationship existing between stone and bread is moreover most worthy of attention.[12] We should point out that the name *Beith-El* applies not only to the place but to the stone itself: 'And this stone, which I have set up as a pillar, shall be God's house.'[13] So it is this stone that must be the true 'divine habitation' (*mishkan*), according to the designation given later to the Tabernacle, that is, the seat of the *Shekinah*. All this is naturally connected to the subject of the 'spiritual influences' (*berakoth*), and when we speak of the 'cult of stones' that was common to so many ancient peoples, it must be understood that this cult was not addressed to the stones themselves but to the divinity whose dwelling-place they were.

The stone representing the *Omphalos* could take the form of a pillar like the stone of Jacob, and it is quite probable that among the Celtic peoples certain 'menhirs' had the same significance; and the oracles were uttered close by these stones, as at Delphi, which is easily explained by the fact that they were considered to be the dwelling-place of the divinity, the 'House of God' being moreover quite naturally identified with the 'Center of the World'. The *Omphalos* could also be represented in the form of a cone, like the black stone of Cybele, or of an ovoid, the cone recalling the sacred mountain,

---

11. The phonetic similarity between *Beith-Lehem* and the form *Beith-Elohim*, which also figures in the text of Genesis, should also be noted.

12. 'And the tempter came and said to him: "If you are the Son of God, command these stones to become loaves of bread"' (Matt. 4:3; cf. Luke 4:3). These words have a mysterious meaning, connected with the following: Christ was indeed to accomplish such a transformation, but spiritually, not materially, as the tempter demanded; now the spiritual order is analogous to the material order, but inversely, and the mark of the demon is to take everything backwards. It is Christ himself who, as a manifestation of the Word, is 'the living bread descended from Heaven,' whence his response: 'Man shall not live by bread alone, but by every word that proceeds from the mouth of God.' In the 'New Covenant' the bread was to be substituted for the stone as the 'House of God'; and what is more, this is why the oracles have ceased. In connection with this bread that is identified with the 'flesh' of the manifested Word, it may be of interest to note also that the Arabic word *lahm*, which is the same as the Hebrew *lehem*, has precisely the meaning of 'flesh', and not 'bread'.

13. Gen. 28:22.

symbol of the 'Pole' or 'World Axis', and the ovoid form relating directly to another, very important, symbol, the 'World Egg'.[14] It should be added that the *Omphalos*, although usually represented by a stone, sometimes took the form of a mound or sort of tumulus, which again is an image of the sacred mountain; thus, in China for example, a mound in the shape of a quadrangular pyramid and formed from the earth of the 'five regions' was formerly raised in the center of every kingdom or feudal state; the four faces corresponded to the four cardinal points and its summit to the center itself.[15] Strangely enough, these 'five regions' are also to be found in Ireland, where the 'standing stone of the chieftain' was raised in a similar way at the center of each domain.[16]

Among Celtic nations it is in fact Ireland that furnishes the most information relative to the *Omphalos*. The country was formerly divided into five kingdoms, of which one bore the name *Mide* (still extant in its anglicized form 'Meath'), from the ancient Celtic word *medion*, 'middle', identical with the Latin *medius*.[17] The kingdom of *Mide*, which had been formed of portions of land appropriated from the other four kingdoms, became the rightful appanage of Ireland's supreme king, to whom the other kings were subordinate.[18] At Ushnagh, situated almost exactly at the center of the country,

14. Sometimes, and notably on certain Greek *Omphaloi*, the stone was encircled by a serpent; this serpent is also found coiled at the base or at the summit of certain Chaldean boundary-stones, which should be considered true 'baetyls'. Moreover, the symbol of the stone, like that of the tree (another figure of the 'World Axis') is in a general way closely connected with the symbol of the serpent, and the same holds true for the symbol of the egg, notably among the Celts and the Egyptians. A remarkable example of the figuration of the *Omphalos* is the 'baetyl' of Kermaria, the general shape of which is that of an irregular cone, rounded at the top, and bearing on one of its faces the sign of the *swastika*. J. Loth, in the work mentioned earlier, provides photographs of this 'baetyl', as well as of other stones of the same kind.

15. The number five has a quite special symbolic significance in the Chinese tradition.

16. *Brehon Laws*, cited by J. Loth.

17. Note too that China is also called the 'Middle Empire'.

18. The capital of the kingdom of *Mide* was *Tara*; now, in Sanskrit the word *Tārā* means 'star', and more particularly the polar star.

there stood a gigantic stone called the 'Navel of the Earth', also called the 'stone of the portions' (*ail-na-meeran*) because it marked the place where the dividing boundaries of the four original kingdoms converged within the kingdom of *Mide*. On the first day of May each year a general assembly was held there very like the annual reunion of the Druids at their 'central consecrated place' (*medio-lanon* or *medio-nemeton*) in Gaul, in the land of the Carnutes, the similarity here with the assembly of the Amphictyons at Delphi being evident.

This division of Ireland into four kingdoms, together with the central region where its supreme ruler resided, is linked to very ancient traditions. It was indeed for this reason that Ireland was called the 'isle of the four Masters',[19] but this name, as well as that of 'green isle' (*Erin*), had previously been applied to another, far more northerly land called *Ogygia*, or rather *Thule*, now unknown and perhaps vanished, but once one of the principal spiritual centers, if not even the supreme one during a certain period. The memory of this 'isle of four Masters' is also found as far away as China, although this seems never to have been noticed before, as witnessed by this Taoist text: 'The emperor Yao took a great deal of trouble, and sincerely believed he had reigned in an ideal way. However, after his visit to the four Masters on the distant island of *Ku-she* [inhabited by 'true men', *chen jen*, that is to say those who have been reintegrated into the 'primordial state'], he realized that he had spoilt everything. The ideal, he discovered, consists of the indifference [or rather the detachment in activity that is non-action] of the superior man[20] who allows the cosmic wheel to turn.'[21] From another point of view, the 'four Masters' are identified with the four *Mahārājas* or 'great kings' who in the Indian and Tibetan traditions

19. The name Saint Patrick, which is usually known only in its latinized form, was originally *Cothraige*, which signifies 'the servant of the four'.

20. The 'true man', being placed at the center, no longer participates in the movement of things, but in reality it is he who directs this movement by his presence alone since the 'Activity of Heaven' is reflected in him.

21. *Chuang Tzu*, chap. 1, Father Weiger translation [in French]. It is said that the emperor Yao reigned in the year 2356 BC.

preside over the four cardinal points, corresponding at the same time to the elements,[22] while the Supreme Master, the fifth, who resides at the center on the sacred mountain, represents the Ether (*Ākāsha*), the 'quintessence' or *quinta essentia* of the Hermeticists, which is the primordial element from which the other four proceed;[23] and analogous traditions are also to be found in Central America.

22. A connection could also be made here with the four *Awtād* of Islamic esoterism.

23. In cruciform figures, such as the *swastika*, this primordial element is also represented by the central point, which is the Pole; the four other elements, as well as the four cardinal points, correspond to the four branches of the cross, symbolizing moreover the quaternary in all of its applications.

10

NAMES AND SYMBOLIC REPRESENTATIONS OF SPIRITUAL CENTERS

As concerns the 'supreme country', many other concordant traditions could be cited, notably its designation by another name that is probably even more ancient than *Paradesha*: this is the name *Tula*, from which the Greeks derived *Thulé*; and, as we have just seen, *Thulé* was probably identical with the original 'isle of the four Masters'. Moreover, this same name *Tula* was given to very diverse regions, so that even today it is still to be found as far afield as Russia and Central America, from which one must doubtless conclude that in some more or less remote age each of these regions was the seat of a spiritual power that was an emanation as it were of that of the primordial *Tula*. We know that the Mexican *Tula* owes its origin to the Toltecs, who, it is said, came from *Aztlan*, the 'land in the midst of the waters' (evidently none other than Atlantis), bringing with them the name *Tula* from their country of origin; the center to which they gave it had probably been intended to replace, in some measure, that of the lost continent.[1] But it is also necessary to distinguish the Atlantean *Tula* and the Hyperborean *Tula*, the latter

---

1. The ideographic sign of *Aztlan* or of *Tula* was the white heron; the heron and the stork play the same role in the West as does the ibis in the East, all three birds figuring among the emblems of Christ. Among the Egyptians, the ibis was one of the symbols of *Thoth*, that is, of Wisdom.

then truly representing the original and supreme center for the totality of the present *Manvantara*; it was this that was the 'sacred isle' par excellence, having originally been situated quite literally at the Pole, as we said above. All the other 'sacred isles', which everywhere bear names of identical meaning, were only its images; and this applies even to the spiritual center of the Atlantean tradition, which only presided over a secondary historical cycle subordinate to the *Manvantara*.[2]

In Sanskrit, the word *Tulā* means 'scales', and denotes more specifically the zodiacal sign of that name [the Scales, or Libra]; there is however a Chinese tradition in which the heavenly Scales were originally the Great Bear.[3] This point is of the greatest importance, for the symbolism attached to the Great Bear is naturally connected in the closest possible way to that of the Pole;[4] but we cannot pursue this question here, for it demands its own special

2. A major difficulty in determining precisely the meeting-point of the Atlantean and the Hyperborean traditions results from various name substitutions which have given rise to multiple confusions; but in spite of everything the question is perhaps not entirely insoluble.

3. The Great Bear is even said to have been called the 'Scales of Jade', jade being a symbol of perfection. Among other peoples the Great Bear and the Little Bear have been assimilated to the two pans of a scale. This symbolic scale is not without connection with one referred to in the *Siphra de-Tzeniutha* (the 'Book of Mysteries', a section of the Zohar): the latter is 'suspended in a place that is not', that is, in the 'non-manifested', which for our world is represented by the polar point; one can say moreover that it is on the Pole that the equilibrium of the world effectively rests.

[In his book *Kabbalah* (various editions) Gershom Scholem transliterates the title as *Sifra de-Ẓeni'uta*, which he translates as 'The Book of Concealment', and which S.L.M. Mathers translates as 'The Book of the Concealed Mystery'. For Guénon's 'suspended in a place that is not', Mathers has 'this equilibrium hangeth in that region which is negatively existent, in the Ancient One.' See S.L. MacGregor Mathers, *The Kabbalah Unveiled* (New York: Samuel Weiser, 1974), p44. See also Guénon's article 'The Siphra de-Tzeniutha' in his *Traditional Forms and Cosmic Cycles*, pt. 3. ED.]

4. In India the Great Bear is the *sapta-riksha*, that is, the symbolic dwelling of the seven *Rishis*; this naturally conforms with the Hyperborean tradition, whereas in the Atlantean tradition the Pleiades, also formed of seven stars, replace the Great Bear in this role; it is known moreover that for the Greeks the Pleiades were the daughters of *Atlas* and, as such, were also called *Atlantides*.

study.[5] There would also be good reason to examine the connection that may exist between the polar Scales and the zodiacal Scales; this latter is regarded, moreover, as the 'sign of Judgement', and what was said previously, in connection with *Melki-Tsedeq*, of the scales as an attribute of Justice makes this name [i.e., Scales or *Tula*] comprehensible as the designation of the supreme spiritual center.

Tula is also called the 'white isle', the color white, as we have seen, representing spiritual authority. In the American [i.e., Amerindian] traditions, *Aztlan* is symbolized by a white mountain, but this symbolism originally applied to the Hyperborean *Tula* and the 'polar mountain'. In India, the 'white isle' (*Shvēta-dvīpa*), which was generally set in the remote regions of the North,[6] is regarded as the 'Abode of the Blessed', which clearly identifies it with the 'Land of the Living'.[7] There is, however, an apparent exception in that Celtic traditions speak specifically of a 'green isle' as the 'isle of the Saints' or the 'isle of the Blessed;[8] in the center of this island there rises the 'white mountain', which is said never to have been submerged in any deluge,[9] and the summit of which is purple in color.[10] This 'mountain of the Sun', as it is also called, is the equivalent of *Meru*, which is the 'white mountain girded in green' by virtue of the fact

5. In connection with what was said earlier concerning the phonetic similarity of *Meru* and *meros*, it is also curious to note that among the ancient Egyptians the Great Bear was called the constellation of the Thigh.

6. *Shvēta-dvīpa* is one of the eighteen subdivisions of the *Jambu-dvīpa*.

7. This also brings to mind the 'Isles of the Blessed' of Western antiquity; but these islands were located in the West (the 'garden of the Hesperides', *hesper* in Greek, *vesper* in Latin, signifying the evening, that is, the West), which indicates a tradition of Atlantean origin, and which from another point of view reminds us of the 'Western Sky' of the Tibetan tradition.

8. The name 'isle of the Saints', as well as 'green isle', was later applied to Ireland, and even to England. Note also that the name of the island of *Heligoland* has the same meaning.

9. Similar traditions concerning the Terrestrial Paradise have already been pointed out. In Islamic esoterism, the 'green isle' (*al jezirah al-khadrah*) and the 'white mountain' (*al-jabal al-abiyad*) are also well known, although very little is said about them to outsiders.

10. We have to do here with the three Hermetic colors—green, white, and red—of which we spoke in *The Esoterism of Dante*.

that it is situated in the middle of the sea,[11] with a triangle of light shining at its summit.

To the various designations of spiritual centers, such as 'white isle' (a designation that like the others could, we repeat, be applied not only to the supreme center, to which it originally appertained, but to secondary centers as well), we must add the names of places, countries, and cities that likewise express the idea of whiteness. These are numerous enough, from Albion and Albania, to Alba Longa, the mother city of Rome,[12] and other ancient cities that may have borne the same name; among the Greeks the name of the city of Argos has the same signification.[13] The reason for these facts will be made clear in what follows.

Something remains to be said about the representation of a spiritual center as an island—one enclosing a 'sacred mountain', moreover—because, while such a location could actually have existed (although not all 'Holy Lands' were islands), it must have a symbolic meaning as well. Historical facts themselves, and especially those of sacred history, in fact translate in their own way truths of a superior order by reason of the law of correspondence that is the

11. It is sometimes also a matter of a girdle of rainbow colors, which can be compared with the sash of *Iris*; Saint-Yves alludes to it in his *Mission de l'Inde,* and the same thing is found in the visions of Anne-Catherine Emmerich. The reader may wish to refer to what was said above on the symbolism of the rainbow, as well as that of the seven *dvīpas.*

12. The Latin *albus,* 'white', can moreover be related to the Hebrew *laban,* which has the same meaning, and whose feminine form *Lebanah* serves to designate the moon; in Latin, *Luna* can mean both 'white' and 'luminous', these two ideas moreover being connected.

13. Between the adjective *argos,* 'white', and the name of the city, there is only a simple difference of accentuation, the name of the city being neuter in gender, whereas Argus is the same word in masculine form. This calls to mind the ship *Argo* (which moreover was said to have been constructed by Argus, and the mast of which was made of an oak from the forest of Dodona); in this case the word may also signify 'swift', this being considered an attribute of light (and especially of lightning), although the primary meaning is 'whiteness' and hence 'luminosity'. Silver [*argent*], which is the white metal and corresponds astrologically to the moon, derives from the same word, the Latin *argentum* and the Greek *arguros* obviously having an identical root.

very foundation of symbolism, and that unites all the worlds in total and universal harmony. The idea evoked by the representation in question is essentially the 'stability' that is also precisely what characterizes the Pole: the island remains immovable amid the ceaseless tossing of the waves, which represents the agitations of the external world; and one must have crossed the 'sea of passions' in order to reach the 'Mount of Salvation', the 'Sanctuary of Peace'.[14]

14. 'The *Yogi*, having crossed over the sea of passions, is united with Tranquillity and possesses the "Self" in its fullness,' says Shankarāchārya (*Atmā-Bodha*). Here the passions are taken to mean all the contingent and transitory modifications that constitute the 'current of forms'; it is the domain of the 'lower waters' according to the symbolism common to all traditions, which is why the conquest of the 'Great Peace' is often represented as a voyage (this being one of the reasons why in Catholic symbolism the Church is represented by a barque); it is also sometimes represented by a war, and the *Bhagavad Gītā* may be interpreted in just this way, as could also the theory of the 'holy war' (*jihād*), according to Islamic doctrine. Let us add that 'walking on the waters' symbolizes domination over the world of forms and change, *Vishnu* being called *Nārāyana*, 'He who walks on the waters'; a connection with the Gospels, where precisely this walking on the waters is reported of Christ, is inevitable here.

11

LOCATION OF
SPIRITUAL CENTERS

In the preceding we have almost entirely left aside the question of the actual location of the 'supreme center', an extremely complex question that is in any case quite secondary from our chosen point of view. There seems good reason to envisage a number of successive locations corresponding to different cycles which are themselves subdivisions of another, more extensive, cycle called the *Manvantara*; moreover, if we were to consider the latter in its totality by placing ourselves outside of time as it were, there would be a hierarchical order to consider among these locations, corresponding to the constitution of traditional forms that are themselves really no more than adaptations of the principal and primordial tradition dominating the entire *Manvantara*. We should recall however that many other centers can exist simultaneously with the principal one, attached to and reflecting it like so many images, and this can easily lead to confusion, especially as these secondary centers, being more outward, are thereby more visible than the supreme center.[1]

In reference to this last point we have already taken particular note of the similarity between Lhasa, the center of Lamaism, and Agarttha. We will now add that even in the West there are at least two cities, Rome and Jerusalem, whose topographical circumstances present peculiarities suggesting a comparable raison d'être (and we

---

1. According to the expression Saint-Yves borrows from the symbolism of the Tarot, the supreme center is to the other centers like the 'closed zero of the twenty-two arcana'.

have already seen that the latter was in effect a visible image of the mysterious *Salem* of *Melki-Tsedeq*). As we have already pointed out, there existed in ancient times what could be called a sacred or sacerdotal geography, and the placement of cities and temples was not arbitrary but determined according to very precise laws;[2] this may give us an inkling of the bonds that unite 'sacerdotal' and 'royal' art to the art of the builders,[3] as well as of the reasons why the ancient guilds possessed an authentic initiatic tradition.[4] Moreover, between the founding of a city and the establishment of a doctrine (or of a new traditional form by adaptation to specific conditions of time and place), there was such a connection that the first was often taken to symbolize the second.[5] Naturally, the most elaborate precautions were taken when fixing the placement of a city destined in one way or another to become the capital of a whole specified part of the world; and the names of such cities would merit careful study, as would also the reported circumstances of their founding.[6]

Without elaborating on questions that are only indirectly related to our present subject, we should nonetheless mention that a center

2. Plato's *Timaeus* appears to contain certain veiled allusions to the science in question.

3. Recall what was said earlier about the title *Pontifex*; moreover, the expression 'Royal Art' has been preserved in modern Masonry.

4. Among the Romans, *Janus* was at once both the god of initiation into the Mysteries and the god of the craft guilds (*Collegia fabrorum*); and this double attribution is particularly significant.

5. We will cite as an example the symbolism of Amphion building the walls of Thebes by the sounds of his lyre; we shall presently see what the name of the city Thebes indicates. The importance of the lyre in Orphism and Pythagorism is well known, but it is interesting to note that in the Chinese tradition musical instruments often play a similar role, which here again must obviously be understood symbolically.

6. Where names are concerned, the preceding discussion has offered several examples, particularly for names connected with the idea of whiteness, and we shall point out a few more. Much could also be said regarding the sacred objects to which the power and even the preservation of the city were linked in certain cases; such were the legendary *Palladium* of Troy, and, in Rome, the shields of the Salii (which were said to have been fashioned from a meteor in the time of *Numa*; the college of the Salii was composed of twelve members); these objects were supports for 'spiritual influences', as was the Ark of the Covenant among the Hebrews.

of the kind just described existed in pre-Hellenic Crete,[7] and that it seems that there were several in Egypt as well (probably founded in successive epochs), such as Memphis and Thebes.[8] The name of the latter, which is also that of a Greek city, is of particular interest as a designation of a spiritual center by reason of its obvious connection with the Hebrew *Thebah*, that is, the Ark of the Deluge. The latter is again a representation of the supreme center, especially in the sense of assuring the preservation of the tradition in a sort of shrouded state[9] during the transitional period between two cycles marked by a cosmic cataclysm that destroys the previous state of the world in order to make place for a new one.[10] The role of the biblical Noah[11] is similar to that played in the Hindu tradition by *Satyavrata*, who, under the name *Vaivasvata*, later became the current *Manu*; but it

7. The name *Minos* is in itself a sufficient indication in this respect, as is *Menes* regarding Egypt; and this brings us back to what was just said about the name *Numa* in connection with Rome, and to the significance of the name *Shlomoh* for Jerusalem.

As concerns Crete, let us in passing point to the use of the *Labyrinth* as a characteristic symbol by the builders of the Middle Ages; and what is curious is that walking the circuit of the labyrinth marked out by paving-stones on the floor of some churches was considered to replace pilgrimage to the Holy Land for those who could not accomplish the latter.

8. We have already seen that Delphi played this role for Greece; the name evokes the dolphin, whose symbolism is very important.

Babylon is another remarkable name, *Bab-Ilu* signifing 'Door of Heaven', which is one of the qualifications attributed to *Luz* by Jacob; moreover, it can also have the meaning 'House of God', as does *Beith-El*; but it becomes synonymous with 'confusion' (*Babel*) when the tradition is lost, being then the reversal of the symbol, *Janua Inferni* taking the place of *Janua Coeli*.

9. This state is assimilable to that represented for the beginning of a cycle by the 'World Egg', which contains in embryo all the possibilities that will develop in the course of the cycle; the Ark likewise contains all the elements that will serve to restore the world, and that are thus the seeds of its future state.

10. Another function of the 'Pontificate' is to assure the passage or transmission of tradition from one cycle to the next, the construction of the Ark having here the same meaning as that of a symbolic bridge since both are equally destined to allow the 'crossing of the waters', which, moreover, has many meanings.

11. It is also noteworthy that Noah is said to have been the first to cultivate the vine (Gen. 9:20), a fact that should be related to what was said earlier on the symbolic meaning of wine and its role in initiatic rites in connection with the sacrifice of Melchizedek.

should be noted that whereas this latter tradition goes back to the beginning of the present *Manvantara*, the biblical Deluge marks only the advent of another, more restricted cycle comprised within this same *Manvantara*:[12] they do not represent the same event, but two analogous ones.[13]

Even more noteworthy is the association that exists between the symbolism of the Ark and that of the rainbow, an relationship suggested in the biblical text by the appearance of the latter after the Deluge as a sign of the covenant between God and earthly creatures.[14] During the cataclysm, the Ark floated on the Ocean of the lower waters; then, at the moment marking the re-establishment of order and the renewal of all things, the rainbow appeared 'in the clouds', that is to say in the region of the upper waters. It is therefore an analogical relationship in the strictest sense, the two figures being inverse and complementary to each other, the convex shape of the ark being directed downward and that of the rainbow upward, so that together they form a complete circular or cyclical figure, of which they comprise as it were the two halves.[15] At the beginning of the cycle this figure was in fact complete: it is the vertical section of a sphere the horizontal section of which is represented by the circular

12. One of the historical meanings of the biblical Deluge can be related to the cataclysm in which Atlantis disappeared.

13. The same remark naturally applies to all the diluvian traditions to be met with among a very great number of peoples, some of which concern still more particular cycles, as is especially the case among the Greeks with the floods of *Deucalion* and *Ogyges*.

14. Gen. 9:12–17.

15. These two halves correspond to those of the 'World Egg', as do the 'upper waters' and the 'lower waters' themselves; during the period of disorder the upper half became invisible, and it was in the lower half that what Fabre d'Olivet calls the 'accumulation of species' took place. Furthermore, the two complementary figures which we are discussing can, from a certain point of view, be compared to two lunar crescents turned inversely toward each other (one being as it were the reflection and symmetrical counterpart of the other with respect to the line separating the Waters), which refers to the symbolism of *Janus*, one of whose emblems moreover is the ship. Also worth remarking is a kind of symbolic equivalence between the crescent, the cup, and the ship, and that the word 'vessel' serves equally to designate the latter two (the 'Holy Vessel' being one of the most frequently used names for the Grail in the Middle Ages).

enclosure of the Terrestrial Paradise;[16] and the latter is divided by a cross formed by the four rivers issuing from the 'polar mountain'. [17] The reconstitution must be accomplished at the end of the same cycle, but then, in the case of the Celestial Jerusalem, the circle is replaced by a square,[18] indicating the accomplishment of what the Hermeticists designated symbolically as the 'squaring of the circle': the sphere, representing the development of possibilities through the expansion of the primordial central point, is transformed into a cube when this development is completed and the final equilibrium for the cycle under consideration is attained.[19]

16. This sphere is again the 'World Egg', the Terrestrial Paradise being situated in the plane that separates it into its upper and lower halves, that is, at the limit between Heaven and Earth.

17. According to the Kabbalists the four letters that form the word *Pardes* correspond to these four rivers; elsewhere we have pointed out their analogical correspondence to the four rivers of hell (*The Esoterism of Dante*, chap. 8).

18. This corresponds to the replacement of plant symbolism by mineral symbolism, the significance of which has been pointed out elsewhere (*The Esoterism of Dante*, chap. 8). The twelve gates of the Celestial Jerusalem naturally correspond to the twelve signs of the zodiac, as well as to the twelve tribes of Israel; it is therefore a question of a transformation of the zodiacal circle following the arresting of the world's rotation and its fixation in a final state, that is, the restoration of the primordial state once the successive manifestation of the possibilities this latter contains will have been completed.

The 'Tree of Life', which was at the center of the Terrestrial Paradise, is likewise at the center of the Celestial Jerusalem, where it bears twelve fruits; and these latter are not without a certain relation to the twelve *Ādityas*, just as the 'Tree of Life' itself has to *Aditi*, the unique and indivisible essence whence they are sprung.

19. One could say that here the sphere and the cube correspond respectively to the dynamic and the static points of view, the six faces of the cube being oriented along the three dimensions of space, as are the six arms of the cross projecting from the center of the sphere. Where the cube is concerned, it is easy to draw a parallel with the Masonic symbol of the 'cubic stone', which likewise has to do with the notion of completion and perfection, that is, with the realization of the plenitude of possibilities implied in a certain state.

12

SOME CONCLUSIONS

ONE CONCLUSION that emerges clearly from the concordant testimonies of all traditions is that there is a 'Holy Land' par excellence, that it is the prototype for all other 'Holy Lands', and that it is the spiritual center to which all others are subordinate. The 'Holy Land' is also the 'Land of the Saints', the 'Land of the Blessed', the 'Land of the Living', and the 'Land of Immortality'; all these expressions are equivalent, and we should add to their number the 'Pure Land',[1] which Plato applies precisely to the 'Abode of the Blessed'.[2] This abode is usually said to be situated in an 'invisible world', but this can only be understood if we do not forget that the same applies to the 'spiritual hierarchies' of which all traditions speak and which in fact represent degrees of initiation.[3]

1. Among the Buddhist schools that exist in Japan there is one, the *Jōdo*, whose name translates as 'Pure Land', recalling the Islamic appellation of the 'Brothers of Purity' (*Ikhwān al-Ṣafā'*), not to mention the *Cathars* of the Western Middle Ages, whose name signifies 'pure'. It is probable moreover that the word *Sufi*, designating Muslim initiates (or, more precisely, those who have reached the final goal of initiation, like the *Yogis* in the Hindu tradition), has exactly the same meaning; in fact, popular etymology, which has it derive from *suf*, 'wool' (of which the clothing worn by the *Sufis* was supposed to be made), is much less satisfactory, and the derivation from the Greek *sophos*, 'sage', while seemingly more acceptable, has the drawback of appealing to a term foreign to the Arabic tongue, so that it seems preferable to accept the interpretation that derives *Sufi* from *ṣafā*, 'purity'.

2. A symbolic description of this 'Pure Land' can be found toward the end of Plato's *Phaedo*; it has already been pointed out that a kind of parallel can be drawn between this description and the one Dante makes of the Terrestrial Paradise (see John Alexander Stewart, *The Myths of Plato* [London: New York: Macmillan, 1905]).

3. Besides, the various worlds are properly states, and not places, although they can be described symbolically as such; the Sanskrit word *loka*, which serves to designate these worlds, and which is identical with the Latin *locus*, contains within

In the present period of our terrestrial cycle, that is, during the *Kali-Yuga*, this 'Holy Land', defended by guardians who keep it hidden from profane view while nevertheless assuring certain exterior relations, is in fact invisible and inaccessible, though only to those who do not possess the necessary qualifications to enter it. Should its location in a definite place then be taken literally, or only symbolically, or as both at the same time? To this we will answer only that, for us, geographical facts as well as historical facts possess, as do all facts, a symbolic import, which obviously takes nothing away from the reality proper to them as such, but rather confers upon them a higher significance in addition to this immediate reality.[4]

We do not claim that we have said all there is to say on the present subject, far from it in fact, for the relationships we have established could assuredly suggest many others; but in spite of everything this study has certainly gone further than any preceding it, and some will perhaps be tempted to reproach us for that. However, we do not believe that too much has been said, and are even persuaded that there is nothing that should not be said, although we are doubtless less disposed than anyone to dispute the fact that there is reason to consider opportuneness when it is a question of making public certain matters of a somewhat unusual character. On the question of opportuneness, only this brief observation need be made: under the circumstances in which we presently live, events unfold with such rapidity that many things, the reasons for which are not immediately obvious, could well find rather unforeseen applications, if not altogether unforeseeable ones, and this sooner than we may wish to

itself the indication of this spatial symbolism. There is also a temporal symbolism, according to which these same states are described under the form of successive cycles, although time, just as much as space, is in reality only a condition proper to one of them, so that the succession is here but an image of a causal chain.

4. This can be compared with the plurality of meanings according to which the sacred texts are interpreted, and which, far from contradicting or destroying, on the contrary complement and harmonize each other, in integral synthetic knowledge. From the point of view indicated here, historical facts correspond to a temporal symbolism, and geographical facts to a spatial symbolism; there is moreover a link or a necessary correlation between them, as there is between time and space themselves, and that is why the location of the spiritual center may be different according to the periods considered.

believe. We wish to refrain from anything that may in any way resemble 'prophesying', but will nevertheless cite here by way of a fitting conclusion the following words of Joseph de Maistre,[5] which are even truer today than they were a century ago: 'We must be ready for an immense event in the divine order, which we are traveling toward with an accelerated speed that must astound all those who watch. Redoubtable oracles have already announced that the time has arrived.'

---

5. *Soirées de Saint-Pétersbourg*, eleventh conversation. To avoid any apparent contradiction with the cessation of oracles alluded to earlier on, and which Plutarch had already observed, we need hardly point out that this word 'oracles' is used by Joseph de Maistre in the very broad sense often given it in ordinary language, and not the proper and precise sense it had in antiquity.

INDEX

Made in the USA
Middletown, DE
04 May 2023

29997507R00066